# In-service training:
# Structure and content

KU-257-834

# In-service training:
# Structure and content

**Editor   Roger Watkins**

**Ward Lock Educational**

ISBN 0 7062 3153 8 hardbound
    0 7062 3154 6 paperback

This collection © Ward Lock Educational 1973

All rights reserved. No part of this book may be reproduced, stored in a retrieval system, or transmitted, in any form or by any means, electronic, mechanical, photocopying, recording or otherwise without the prior permission of the copyright owner.

Set in 10 on 11 point Linotype Pilgrim
by Willmer Brothers Limited, Birkenhead
for Ward Lock Educational
116 Baker Street, London WIM 2BB
Made in England

# Contents

Preface  7
*Lord Boyle*

Introduction  9
*Roger Watkins*

1 The James Report's third cycle  12
*Lord James*

2 Teachers and in-service training  19
*Edward Britton*

3 In-service training provision: LEAS  33
*John Taylor*

4 In-service training provision: colleges of education  41
*Stanley Hewett*

5 In-service training provision: polytechnics  49
*Eric Robinson*

6 In-service training provision: universities  60
*Geoffrey Mattock*

7 Meeting teachers' needs  68
*Brian Cane*

8 The role of the school in in-service training  81
*Roger Watkins*

9 Strategies of curriculum change   91
*Eric Hoyle*

10 The diffusion of Schools Council curriculum development
   projects   104
*Tony Light*

11 Local curriculum development   113
*Allan Rudd*

The contributors   125

# Preface

## Lord Boyle

It is safe to say that of all the recommendations contained in the James Report, none has received more widespread endorsement than the proposal for a massive increase of provision for in-service, or 'third cycle', training.

There are many reasons for the current dissatisfaction with the situation as it exists at present. The provision for in-service training is still relatively small. Too many of the courses relate to a limited number of 'fashionable' subjects. There are not enough practical courses on topics like school and class organization. It is often difficult for teachers to obtain release from school in order to attend, and their costs are not always fully reimbursed. Too many courses, again, involve travelling a considerable distance from home, and the premises are often inadequate.

Surprisingly little is known about the effectiveness of courses, and it is important that any extension in their number should be accompanied by a far greater effort at evaluation. Up to now, in-service training has operated mainly for individual teachers; but if we want to see real changes and improvements in the curriculum, it becomes necessary to retain whole schools, or at least whole departments. I also believe (as do a number of my colleagues at Leeds University) that we must be prepared to reconsider the use of the long vacation for extensive retraining of this kind.

There are two particular examples of the use of in-service training which seem to me to deserve special mention. The first concerns secondary school reorganization. By 1974, there will be at least fifty middle school schemes operating within local education authorities, and a smaller (but by no means negligible) number of schemes involving sixth form colleges. Surely it will be of great importance to spread more widely what appear to be the best existing practices in relation to each kind of scheme. Second, our increasingly multiracial and multicultural society already requires us to look very closely at the teaching materials being used in our schools—and this does not only apply to schools in 'immigrant' areas.

Everyone is agreed that the Open University will be a most important source of in-service training in the future. But I believe that other universities, too, will have a major part to play. Already universities and colleges are providing a considerable fraction of the total of longer courses. Universities have a distinctive contribution to make because of their national responsibility for assessing the current position with regard to any intellectual discipline, as well as their traditional concern for academic reliability and rigorous standards.

Equally, I am certain that many of those who teach in universities will themselves have much to gain from a closer involvement with in-service training, and the extra understanding of the current concerns of the education service which this involvement will bring.

Edward Boyle 1972

# Introduction

The White Paper *Education: A Framework for Expansion* published in December 1972 included in its package the Government's proposals for the restructuring of teacher training. Many of these had been formulated in one form or another in the debate on how we should best prepare entrants for the rapidly changing profession of education, a debate in which interested parties have been engaged since the third enquiry of the Select Committee on Education and Science, which was set up by the Labour Government in 1968. The evidence given to this Committee was included in that collected and studied by Lord James and his Committee which reported on *Teacher Education and Training* in January 1972 (DES) in an atmosphere of intense speculation. This document immediately became a Green Paper and acted as the basis for further discussion and negotiation which even now has not been brought to an end by the appearance of the White Paper. In such a comparatively brief document, packed as the White Paper is with declarations of intent, Mrs Thatcher could hardly do more than sketch the main lines of her policy for teacher education. In many ways negotiations about all important detail are only just beginning and although one major proposal has come through unchallenged — the provision of in-service education for teachers on a greatly increased scale — many aspects of this revolutionary development in the profession have still to be settled.

In-service training was the subject of a national conference held in Leeds in July 1972. It has often been remarked that seldom could so many people be in favour of a development of which we all know so little. Commitment to the further professional education of teachers constitutes an act of faith which must now be given some substance in the reality of experience. I do not think it too much to claim that the Leeds conference was a major step in this process. Although the contributors were speaking before the publication of the

White Paper, their remarks have great relevance to the discussion which has ensued.

The speakers in many ways selected themselves as being leading figures in the field or representative of important interests. Their contributions to the conference, in some cases prepared as papers, in other cases edited from tape-recordings, are gathered in this volume and speak largely for themselves. Not represented here are the many discussions, formal and informal, which took place and the questions put by the audience which helped to sharpen many of the points made by speakers. This audience drawn from LEAS, colleges of education and institutes of education, teachers centres, teachers' professional associations, polytechnics and the DES was invited to form a cross-section of professional involvement. The willingness of the members of the audience to participate, sometimes vigorously, contributed much to the success of the conference.

However in the process of sending out invitations a curious situation emerged. Very few of the bodies represented had people appointed with a clearly defined responsibility for in-service training. This was particularly so in the case of LEAS. Perhaps the first step to the expansion of in-service training would be to establish clear lines of communication within and between the bodies involved. Responsibility for in-service training is too important to be left floating uneasily between administrators and tutors. It will be a major responsibility of the new regional machinery to ensure coordination. It is clear from experience already gained and described by Geoffrey Mattock in his paper that the avoidance of wasteful duplication of effort depends on the efficient sharing of information and on the acceptance of responsibility. Tutors too will have to become wholeheartedly committed. Edward Britton in his contribution makes a convincing case against part-time organizers of in-service training and argues persuasively that it will have to become a form of adult professional education in its own right. Mrs Thatcher's White Paper provides the real basis for a professional *éducation permanente*.

We sensed at the conference some of the incipient competition between LEAS on the one hand and the colleges and universities on the other for control of the content of in-service training. John Taylor makes a strong case for LEAS to be wholly involved in in-service training not only because they are the paymaster but because they have a responsibility for the implementation of an educational policy in their area and the responsibility for ensuring continuity of schools' work when teachers are seconded for in-service training. Stanley Hewett was prepared to concede a powerful representation of LEAS on a controlling regional organization but warned against allowing them to become dominant as the danger was that this might lead to LEAS providing only those courses which suited their particular objectives in the running of their education services.

Heeding Eric Robinson's fears about 'overorganization', the conference moved on to consider the nature of the training which should be offered to teachers with some years experience. We acknowledged that further professional education has its own distinctive characteristics, that it was not simply more of that which was given in preservice training, but we also recognized that we have a long way to go in devising those modes of education which a teacher will find most helpful in his work. The situation is further complicated, as Tony Light pointed out in his paper, by the fact that 'development and training are inextricably bound together'. The curriculum development process is itself an in-service training experience of the most intense kind and once the process has been completed its conclusions and benefits need to be communicated to teachers in such a way that those in no way connected with a project come to share the insights which the project team have experienced. In this the role of the in-service tutor or the leader of local curriculum development is crucial. In Allan Rudd's phrase, they are responsible for providing those circumstances likely to foster 'emerging professional maturity', and Rudd describes the circumstances which experience in the north-west suggests have been most successful.

Excellent work over the years has been done in the overlapping fields of curriculum development and in-service training, much of it based on local experience and intuition. But as Brian Cane's research and his paper at the conference indicates, there are still fundamental questions to which we are seeking an answer, for example do we possess an adequate body of professional knowledge that can be communicated to teachers through in-service education? As the work expands it is to be hoped that it will develop an organizing theory which will draw on related experience in all fields of professional education. Eric Hoyle's paper was particularly welcomed at the conference because it provided a strategic overview which enabled in-service training tactics to be planned with regard to as many as possible of the variables in the whole complex pattern.

It was demonstrated beyond doubt at the Leeds conference that there was great goodwill toward the development of in-service training and a willingness to plan the future together. I hope that the papers in this volume will be of value to all involved in this urgent and exciting task.

Roger Watkins

# 1 The James Report's third cycle

## Lord James

I am very glad indeed for several reasons that the Leeds Institute arranged a conference on in-service training. The first is that of all the parts of the Report of the Committee on the Education and Training of Teachers (DES 1972), the recommendations on in-service training have been those most generally welcomed, which gave us the chance of discussing what ought to happen and what may, indeed, happen in the next five or six years, in an atmosphere free of the controversy and even acrimony that has been associated with some of our other proposals. Second, the first and I think in some ways the most important of our conclusions, was that an entirely new scope and emphasis must be given to in-service training. We felt this so strongly that we did, as it were, write our report backwards, and actually began it with the education and training of the serving teacher. This was not simply a gimmick: it was a measure of the importance which we attached to this aspect of the problem. To ascribe such a priority to this element involved to some extent an act of faith, for surprisingly little hard information exists as to what effects various kinds of postexperience training actually have on teaching and the teacher: how long these effects last, what are the most appropriate kinds of education to accomplish ends which may be quite different for different individuals and what effect on the schools themselves the in-service education of their staff has. One could think of many more questions to which we badly need answers.

In view of what I have said about how little we really know about the effectiveness of postexperience training it may seem perverse that we gave it the prominence which we did. We did that partly because of this belief which we nearly all share, partially unsubstantiated though it is, that such training is a good thing in itself, but partly also because the content of initial training will be radically different if we can be confident that some topics can be safely omitted because those omissions can be rectified in subsequent years, and indeed in some cases can be deferred with positive advantage. It would be a remarkable piece of self-deception if we believed that the preparation of a student for any of the great variety of tasks that we include under the word 'teacher' could be completed in two or three or four years. And of course we do not. The multiplicity of courses for serving teachers arranged in this country by the Department of Education and Science, by local authorities, by university departments and institutes, and by professional associations of teachers of very various kinds, all bear witness to the efforts that are already being made. Where do they need improvement? Many of them are too short for their declared aims; many suffer from the financial obstacles put in the way of the organizers and the teachers who might wish to participate; we have in many cases no idea how effective they are, and finally they are often lacking in machinery for coordination so that wasteful duplication occurs and important gaps exist. But having said that, it was certainly no part of our intention to do anything but expand, encourage and improve the kind of courses that already exist. What we did affirm is the need for the teacher to have a *right* to a more substantial period of in-service education. Our suggestion is for one term in seven years which we hope will improve to five years.

We have been asked one question. Should not obligation go with rights and should not such a term be compulsory? I may say that we devoted much thought to this question of leaving it for the time being as a voluntary provision. Does this not mean, it may be asked, that the very teachers who need it most will not, in fact, go on the courses? I will not go into the arguments that brought us to our conclusion. They included such considerations as the undesirable effect of unwilling conscripts on courses during what will inevitably be a time of experiment and transition.

A second question that arose was whether, if courses were not to be compulsory, some financial inducement should not be given to those who attend them in the way of increments. We preferred to leave the inducement as being primarily one of becoming better at one's job, and leaving more materialist considerations to be dealt with by the ordinary mechanism of promotion of more highly qualified people. Let me turn now from the general principle of the desirability of in-service education to enumerate some of the very varying factors which make it so vital.

First it is necessary because knowledge changes. I will take the first example that occurs to me—myself. I took my degree in chemistry in 1930. If I look at the papers set in the same examination today I cannot do them : that would not be expected. But the real point is that I never *could* have done them, because two-thirds of the knowledge required actually did not *exist* at the time. And some of that knowledge is now part of the school curriculum. Thus although during my first twelve years as a schoolmaster I could still teach the top sixth form, during my sixteen years as a headmaster I was relegated to teaching one particular branch of chemistry to the B stream, and now I could not teach a sixth form at all. Given a term in a university learning some modern chemistry, I could just about make an attempt. That is an example at one end of the academic spectrum, the highly specialized work of a good sixth form. But if we think of the other end, the greater knowledge of how five year olds learn that we have acquired over the past years, are we not driven to the conclusion that the infant or primary teacher no less needs refreshment, if of a quite different kind? It is quite certain that the junior school teacher who teaches arithmetic and who qualified ten years ago has never heard of set theory. Whether it is right that they should now is another question, but the fact is that many think it desirable that they should, and the only way they can learn it is to have time off to do so.

But this leads us to the next point. Not only does knowledge change: techniques of teaching change. The changes may involve whole questions of attitude—associated with team teaching, or open plan schools or whatever. They may involve the more material affairs that are included in the words educational technology. The idea that the mere installation of a language laboratory will revolutionize the teaching of primary French is a heresy extraordinarily widely held. If we devise new tools for teachers it is vital that they should be given really wisely planned courses on their value and their limitations, courses which are cheaper than the actual hardware which without them is almost useless.

And third, society changes. The growth of technology produces new problems and if our citizens are to be aware of them and be prepared to cope with them, then fresh demands are inevitably placed on those who teach. We are in many ways becoming more humane, and some special training is therefore necessary for those who teach in educational priority areas, or whatever we call them. The challenges of a multiracial society have educational results. If the character of the society for which he prepares his pupils changes radically during his working life, it is clearly essential that the teacher shall have periodical refreshment.

And teachers themselves change. They both tend to ossify and to develop. The mere avoidance of staleness is one of the great justifications for in-service training. Hence we must avoid rigidity in our plans for what teachers should actually do in their periods away from their schools. The chance to follow a course of wide reading and to talk about it with tutors and colleagues may be the right shot in the arm that some need. The opportunity to engage in some modest piece of research may be the right thing for others. The mere opportunity to associate in the life of a college, a different school or group of schools, a university department or an education office, may provide the stimulus that will give some stale teachers a new lease of life.

Further, it is clear that with experience some teachers develop new interests in special fields, for example, the teaching of handicapped children of various kinds, school library work, or counselling. All these demand special skills and it is one of the functions of in-service training to provide them. The man or woman who becomes a head of a department, or of a school, will meet their new responsibilities better if they have some specific preparation for them.

At the moment we do too little to prepare teachers for such changes of function. To take myself again as an example. When I became a headmaster twenty-seven years ago I was fortunate enough to be serving under a man who was himself a great headmaster, Spencer Leeson. He regarded it as his duty to prepare me for my new responsibility by discussion and by writing a remarkable document for me, which I still regard as the best short guide to a headmaster's job. But I was quite exceptionally fortunate, and I do not believe that we should leave this kind of preparation to the chance that a future headmaster may be working under a great man. We should devise courses which will help him to face new problems and wider responsibilities, even if they are less inspiring than the informal help that I was fortunate enough to receive.

Not only do teachers change, but schools change also. A teacher imbued with the ideas and ideals of a highly selective system stands in need of time for reflection, study and discussion when he is faced with the problems of widely mixed ability groups in a comprehensive school which may well be a much larger community than any he has encountered.

Finally, in-service education and training can do much to bridge the gap in communication which tends to develop in our educational system. New methods, new curricula and new attitudes evolve by the research and development sponsored by the Schools Council, Nuffield and other such agencies. But one is conscious that too few of these advances find their way into the actual classroom. It is only through the growth of in-service training that this gulf between advancing knowledge and practice can be bridged.

These are some of the obvious kinds of in-service education and some of the very various objectives that it must pursue. It is quite clear that if even some of them are to be followed up, a very wide variety of institutions will be involved. To bring me up to date in my chemistry I should probably go to a university or polytechnic and take a joint course run by the departments of education and chemistry. If I am interested in backward readers I should go to a college of education or a university department that specializes in this field. If my school has gone comprehensive on some particular pattern the right place with which to be associated may be a professional centre in some suitable area, where programmes of study visits and seminars are provided. The concept of professional centres, whether in colleges or university departments of education or polytechnics, or unattached to any of these, implies a degree of collaboration between those engaged in the education of teachers that we have not yet seen. Far from creating barriers in education, a truly bold programme of in-service education would be a solvent of divisions. This is not to say that every professional centre must try to do too much, or all do the same things. I think that we can without too much imagination envisage the emergence of acknowledged centres of excellence in various fields to which teachers who wished to use their term of in-service education to follow a particular line would naturally gravitate. I can think, for example, of three such fields where it would be appropriate for a teacher to come to York; for a number of other fields we would be quite unsuitable.

Two very important but more material topics must be mentioned. The first is finance. Argument is still proceeding as to how much a full programme of in-service education would cost. It is, in fact, not as simple a sum to do as might appear. One complicating factor is the considerable number of teachers who do not stay long enough in the profession to qualify for a term away. The second complication concerns the number of those who do unfortunately stay, but who would not want to undergo a voluntary scheme to take advantage of the opportunities offered, a number that one hopes will diminish. Thirdly, there is the question of geographical distribution, linked with the home-based accessibility of certain kinds of course. But preliminary estimates do indicate that the cost of the proposals would not be prohibitively great, if we believe it to be, as I am sure we must, a vitally important line of advance. In particular I am encouraged that some knowledgeable educators who are also guardians of the public purse, like Sir William Alexander, are enthusiastic for the kind of massive development of in-service education of which we are talking.

The second area in which we shall have a series of intractable problems is, of course, in staffing. If in-service education is to become a reality on any significant scale, one preliminary and essential condition must be recognized: what we consider the normal staffing ratio for schools must take adequate account of it. If $x:1$ is a reasonable staffing ratio, then we must budget for $x-y:1$ if in-service training is to be a reality. But we do know that staffing is not simply a question of overall numbers: it is also a question in many cases of specialized skills. The replacement of certain kinds of teacher during periods of absence will obviously be a perpetual headache for heads and administrators. What we must beware of is the kind of attitude that foresees the difficulties and uses them as an excuse for doing nothing. There are means of meeting many of these difficulties, through having a pool of peripatetic teachers, or through recalling those who have left the profession through marriage or retirement and who, while not being prepared for a permanent job, would nevertheless be prepared to stand in for a term or so. It is not impossible that the term of in-service education could for some people be an exchange with someone in a college who would themselves benefit from a return to the classroom. There is the newly qualified teacher who might well contemplate a series of short-term posts to widen his experience. These are some possibilities: there are, no doubt, many others that will emerge as the problems become clearer. But as I have said, the fact that some of these suggestions are not fully satisfactory, that one can foresee the need for expedients and improvisation, must not deter us if we really put in-service education as high on our list of priorities as did my committee. Such expedients and improvisations will no doubt put additional burdens on the teachers in our schools. I believe they will cheerfully carry them if they realize that they are thereby contributing to the long-term welfare of the schools and of their own profession. Obviously refreshed teachers abreast of advancing knowledge, whether of their specialist subjects, or the methodology of teaching it, will contribute to the first of these objectives. In my view it is no less clear that the claim that ours is a profession demanding a lifelong process of thought and education, will contribute to the teacher's own self-esteem. But let me conclude by emphasizing once again certain conditions. In-service education will only be worth the personal and financial sacrifices that it will involve if it is based on collaboration of the closest kind between the various agencies concerned, resulting in a coordination between their efforts. It demands, moreover, a programme of investigation and evaluation of the methods most appropriate for the very different tasks which such education must fulfil. And finally it calls for a resolution that refuses to allow obvious difficulties and manifest sacrifices to be excuses for inaction in an enterprise which can ultimately affect in the most radical way the education and hence the lives of those we teach.

*References*
DES (1972) *Teacher Education and Training* (James Report) London: HMSO

# 2 Teachers and in-service training

## Edward Britton

I intend to discuss the question of in-service training from the point of view of the teachers. What I am going to say represents a purely personal point of view; it is not necessarily the view of the National Union of Teachers. The Union has done a great deal of work on this matter, and has indeed published various documents, but what follows is a personal point of view, since it covers some matters on which the Union has not as yet adopted firm policy.

It was apparent when the James Report was published that only the proposals concerning in-service training were received with anything approaching universal approbation. It has already been said that in-service training, as referred to by the James Committee, is a matter of faith. This is obvious because virtually none of it takes place at the present time. There are, I believe, a total of about 800 teachers who are seconded for a one year full-time course at any one time and a further total of about 200 who are on three month short courses. This means in a year there is a total of about 1,400 teachers who undertake either a year's course or a three months' course. In other words, there are about 1,400 per annum who are doing the sort of thing that James proposes.

A little arithmetic will indicate that if every existing teacher were to have the present opportunity for in-service training of the James type, we would give the existing teaching force one course in about 250 years. Those who were at the end of the queue and had to wait well into the twenty-third century for their turn might by that time not be particularly interested in the information that was being put to them. I point this out because John Taylor's chapter will give a picture of a local authority that is only too anxious to provide the kind of course that James was thinking of but which teachers are not prepared to attend.

I think that possibly John Taylor has a measure of right on his side but I would like him to look at the city of Leeds and do the sort of calculation that I have just done nationally and find out when, at the present rate, he would be likely to provide in-service training for all the teachers in his city. The fact that this also, I suspect, would be in the nature of 250 years from now indicates that there is a good deal more in this business than meets the eye.

I would agree in general terms with Lord James's analysis of the need for varying types of course. There is the need to keep up to date with subject knowledge. This does not merely apply to the sciences, in which knowledge is growing phenomenally fast. It is equally true of the arts, where there has been as much growth as there has been in the understanding of the physical sciences. It is just as important for the teacher of history or English literature or any other subject to have the opportunity to keep his knowledge up to date.

There is also the need to keep abreast with changing teaching techniques. One cannot rely on the colleges of education to ensure that the teaching profession is up to date even with the use of the ironmongery. If one were to be content to do that, it would take forty years before every teacher knew how to operate a film projector. Quite clearly the new techniques should be available to the existing teaching force and therefore they must be taught as part of in-service training. This is just as true of teaching methods as of ironmongery.

There also is need for teachers to be kept up to date with school organizational changes. One thing that is quite apparent from a good deal of research that has been done on comprehensive education is that the comprehensive school does not work if it is staffed with people who either do not believe in comprehensive education or, if they do believe in it, do not understand the implications of the new school organization.

As Lord James indicated, some subjects require a measure of maturity on the part of the teacher if they are to be successfully taught. I think many of us would go along with him when he says that you cannot give students in colleges of education the ability to advise on careers or on the personal problems of children in schools. They have neither the personal maturity nor the experience to be able to assimilate that kind of teaching while they are still at college. Similarly there are new subjects in schools. French in primary schools is just one example. All these require a good deal of in-service training for the teaching profession if they are to be satisfactorily taught.

Then the question of actual change of job on the part of the teacher must be considered. The necessity of giving headteachers training in their job is apparent to anybody who has been appointed as a headteacher. Every head knows from his own bitter experience how lonely and difficult the first few years can be. Looked at purely from the point of view of the mechanics of the job, anyone who has visited schools and seen how severely teachers and children may suffer day after day from an incompetent timetable, must be amazed that so little is done to instruct either the headteacher, or the person who composes the timetable, in the elements of what a timetable involves. I suspect that one of the reasons for this is that very few people in university departments or colleges of education have any personal knowledge of how to prepare a timetable for a large present-day secondary school.

There is also the fact that many teachers find themselves at some point in their career either teaching a subject, or in a part of the education system, for which they were not trained. This is particularly true of married women who take jobs in schools because the schools are near their homes and not because the school provides the sort of job for which they were trained; and this is not in any way to under-estimate the immense value of the married women who have returned to teaching.

There is also the need for a teacher to have a knowledge of the rest of the educational system. It is impossible to teach really well in a secondary school unless you know what happens in the primary school and equally impossible to teach really well in a primary school unless you have some ideas of what the pupils are going on to in the secondary school. Consequently teachers need to learn about developments that are taking place in other parts of the system beside their own.

I need not expand upon this except for the one point which I feel Lord James completely underestimated in his paper when he talked about a teacher whose knowledge was not up to date being able to teach the B stream in the sixth form rather than the A stream. The implication was that if the pupils have a relatively low intellectual ability in terms of their subject, it is not important for the teacher to know the subject well. This is based on a completely false under-standing of the teaching situation. I am pretty certain that no one here would suggest that if you are teaching music to an A stream in a sixth form (probably the sixth form does not do music, but that is beside the point) you need to have an LRAM, whereas if you are teaching music to form 4E, or wherever the failures of the present system congregate, all you need is to be able to pick out a hymn tune with one finger on the piano. Quite obviously, music is a subject which it is just as important to know well whatever children you are teaching.

But this is true of all subjects. It is easy enough to hold the interest of A streamers in English literature even if the only poems you know are those in the *Golden Treasury*. But if you have to teach English literature to a fourth year D or E stream, there are perhaps only two or three poems in the English language that will catch their imagination and you have to know your English literature sufficiently well to be able to spot these two or three poems. You must also know the children sufficiently well to be able to predict which poems will engage their interest, but if you do not know the poems you are sunk. From my own experience I believe that when teachers slip up really seriously in their teaching it is more often as a result of a lack of subject knowledge than lack of anything else. I am not saying that because you know your subject well you will therefore be a good teacher. We have all come across the brilliant academic who just cannot get his subject across to the children, but equally I believe that nobody who does not know his subject can teach well.

The role of in-service training in enabling the teacher to become better acquainted with his subject should not be underestimated. The normal pattern for in-service training is not the first class honours graduate whose subject has progressed since he left college; it is the teacher who some years ago took a major subject in a three-year, or even two-year, course in a college of education. Indeed, a very common pattern will be the teacher who is teaching a subject which he did not even take as a major subject at his college of education. There is therefore a real need for opportunities for teachers to improve their subject knowledge, a fact which is clearly indicated by the options that teachers are making in Open University courses.

Having made these preliminary points, I would like to point out that certain things flow from the James Committee's recommendations. First, what I regard as being the basis of his recommendations. The Committee is recommending that every teacher should undertake the equivalent of one term, full-time, in-service training in every seventh year. This one term need not necessarily be one whole term at one time. It can be made up of periods of shorter duration, but if so they must be substantial periods. The Committee is thinking in terms of not less than four weeks in one continuous stretch.

Now, what are the implications of these recommendations? Let us first look at the size of the operation. One term in seven years, or in other words one term in twenty-one terms, means that one teacher in twenty will be away from school on a course at any one time. We have, all told, a teaching force of about 350,000, so this means that at any one time there would be 17,500 teachers out of school undertaking full-time courses of one month or possibly longer. Now this by any reckoning is quite a substantial number.

Here I ought to refute a myth that the James Committee appears to subscribe to, namely that the teaching profession is quite substantially made up of people who are, so to speak, in-and-outers, people who come into teaching for a year or two and then disappear. This is not true. Mathematics, just like chemistry, has changed since 1930, but a little pre1930 arithmetic will indicate that if 50 per cent of students in colleges stay in teaching for only one year, and the remaining 50 per cent stay for a lifetime, then at any one point in time 95 per cent of the active teaching profession will be made up of teachers who are in teaching for a lifetime. What happens is that the in-and-outers represent a constantly changing fringe and the large number of new students coming out of the colleges each year largely go to replace the in-and-outers who have been in and gone out again in quite a short space of time. The large majority of the teaching profession teach for substantial periods of their lives and you cannot detract from the 17,500 who will be undertaking full-time in-service training by saying that only a small proportion of teachers will teach for seven years, and therefore qualify for an in-service term. The in-service training of teachers must therefore be a highly planned operation.

It is attractive to think that in-service training might be done in universities during university vacation time, but you cannot have a system under which no teachers will be out of school during the autumn term, or the spring term, but the full year's quota, i.e. 52,500, will be out in the summer term. Quite clearly, the release of teachers must be spread evenly across the whole of the academic year and this implies that in-service training will be undertaken in premises and with staff whose job it is to deal with in-service training. I am not saying that those premises may not be attached to some other educational institution, but it is quite ludicrous to think in terms of dealing with in-service education of teachers on the basis that it can take place in colleges of education or universities at times when the buildings are not required for the purpose for which they were built. Nor can it be provided by staff whose basic job is providing some other form of education. Certainly there can be give and take. One would expect there to be an interchange of staff between colleges of education concerned with initial training and the staff who are responsible for the teaching side of in-service training. But it is not feasible for the in-service training of teachers to be mainly staffed by the teaching staff of colleges of education, universities or polytechnics at those times when they are not required to undertake teaching of the students with whom their institution is primarily concerned. The in-service training of teachers will have to become a form of adult professional education in its own right.

Let us now return to the question of releasing teaching staff from schools, because this is the key to the whole situation. The difficulty of releasing staff is the main reason, if not the only reason, why we are told that there are plenty of courses available but no teachers volunteer to go to them. Most people readily appreciate the difficulty of releasing staff from a small primary school with only two or three teachers in all. If a school is asked to release one of their total of three teachers they are being asked to forego 33 per cent of their teaching strength and this is more than one has the right to ask of any staff. But it is assumed by many people that the situation is much easier in large secondary schools. Superficially a school with forty staff—and it doesn't have to be a very big school these days to have forty staff—can quite easily release one of them. To release teachers to comply with the James proposals would mean that such a school would permanently have to release between six and seven teachers, but quite apart from that, in practice it is often more difficult for a secondary school of this size to release a single teacher than it is for a primary school to do so. In primary schools education in the main is based on general purpose teaching. One teacher teaches right across the board. It is relatively easy to obtain a supply teacher who is a general purpose teacher to replace the teacher who has been released (though to some extent it depends upon the district in which you live). But if, in a secondary school, you want a woodwork teacher to go on a three month course, it is no good replacing him with a teacher of classics or English literature. He must be replaced by a woodwork teacher. Unless the school is exceptionally large, if the woodwork teacher is to be released that school will have to give up not one third of its woodwork staff, but its entire woodwork staff. Unless another woodwork teacher is provided there will be virtually no woodwork teaching in the school for the three months that the normal teacher is away on a course. And this applies to a greater or less extent to all secondary school subjects. The secondary school has to give up, in effect, a very large proportion of the subject staff to let somebody go on a course; and if the teacher is conscientious about his teaching, the teacher himself will refuse to go on a course, even if the headteacher is cooperative. The result is that relatively few people volunteer to go to the courses that already exist.

So the implication of Lord James's proposals is that each local education authority will deliberately have to plan replacement of their teachers during the periods that they are released for in-service education, and do so on the basis that the children's education does not suffer. In other words, not only will the local authority have to appoint a supply staff to be available to replace the teachers concerned, but supply staff will have to be planned in relation to the subject specializations that are required in the schools. This means that it will not be enough to rely upon supply teachers who will come in casually when they are needed; it implies that there will be a permanent full-time supply staff, planned to contain so many woodwork teachers, so many music teachers and so on, through all the specializations.

Moreover, the release of staff from the schools will also have to be planned. If, for instance, the permanent supply staff contains only two woodwork specialists, it is no good allowing the woodwork specialist in every school in the county to go off on a woodwork course at the same time. Otherwise we would be back at square one. Two people would be able to be replaced and the rest of the schools would have to forego their woodwork teaching.

The James proposals, therefore, involve considerable planning. Such planning would depend upon having someone to undertake it which implies, as I see it, some form of committee with responsibility for the overall planning, together with some kind of administrative staff to be responsible for the organization of the committee and carrying out the committee's intentions. Incidentally, no committee of this kind will work satisfactorily unless it contains a number of teachers and unless it is something more than an advisory committee whose advice can be taken or ignored as somebody outside the committee thinks fit.

These seem to be some of the implications of the James proposals. But much more detailed planning on a national basis is also involved. Where the specialist subjects are concerned there is need for an overall national planning of courses. Moreover, the specialist subjects are not necessarily restricted to secondary schools, for there are specialist aspects of primary teaching, particularly in special education, that are just as important and just as much in need of in-service training.

I now want to deal with the question of compulsion versus incentive. Here again, it is not clear what the James proposals imply, for the simple reason that we have very little experience. It is easy to denigrate the kind of financial incentive that exists in some parts of America, where attendance at some often very strange courses can qualify a teacher to receive salary increases; but I am not sure that because, by repute, credit marks are given in America for in-service courses which we would not consider to be educationally valid, there is therefore sound reason for rejecting a similar system in this country. Indeed I sometimes wonder whether the people who are so very supercilious about the American system of increasing salaries by means of credits for attending courses ever look seriously into the reasons why in some schools in this country teachers are appointed to above-scale posts. I suspect that our own domestic situation might not stand up to examination by an unfriendly critic.

Nevertheless, I personally am not opposed to the idea of compulsion. Pupils have to attend under compulsion, and therefore teachers are presumably prepared to justify compulsion. There seems to be a certain illogicality in their position if they are not prepared to submit to some compulsion themselves. But I see compulsion not so much as imposing a duty upon the teacher as giving the teacher a safeguard against the dilatory local authority and employer. Indeed when you think about the compulsion imposed upon children in the classroom you know perfectly well that if that compulsion were not there the education would not be available at all. It is very easy for an authority first of all to fail to provide suitable education, and then, because nobody turns up for it voluntarily, (nobody turns up for the nonexistent) to argue that there is no demand.

We have only to turn to the sad history of day release in further education, or look at the nonimplementation of the county college provision that was promised in the 1944 Act, or look at the Henniker-Heaton report and its very hopeful forecast of the growth in day release, and then look at the actuality, to realize that the voluntary principle does not always work. There are fewer students enjoying day release in 1972 than there were in 1962. In the light of this experience it is clear that compulsion is not so much something that is imposed upon the student as something that is imposed upon the provider of courses and upon the employer to force him to release the student. I suspect a little cynically that provision of in-service training along the lines of the James Report will not be made unless there is a measure of compulsion on the part of the teacher, for such compulsion implies a compulsion on the part of the local education authority to make the necessary provision.

When the NUT went to discuss the James Report with the representatives of the DES, the question of compulsion was raised and it was quite clear that the DES was thinking very differently from the teachers concerning compulsion. The DES, and I suspect local authorities as well, regard compulsion as being the right of the local authority, or possibly an HMI, to say to a teacher: 'You will attend such and such a course in such and such a place at such and such a time.' The NUT would resist this interpretation most strongly. It would be a quite unjustifiable imposition upon the teacher. What we should have is not merely the right to attend a course of in-service training one term in every seven years, but the contractual necessity to undertake attendance one term in seven years.

The teacher himself should have considerable rights in the choice of the course he attends. Undue pressure on the part of either central or local government authority could be dealt with by the teachers' organizations in exactly the same way that we deal with other unsatisfactory conditions of service at the present moment. But unless there is a measure of compulsion I suspect that we shall continue to have local authorities saying that they are only too willing to provide courses for which there is a demand, but excusing themselves from actually providing them by pointing to the fact that there is no demand; and there would be no demand simply because the conditions under which teachers would have to attend the courses were unreasonable.

A further point arises from this that has not been looked at carefully. The question of part-time versus full-time courses and the question of residence have both been raised tentatively, but have not been examined in detail. Let us deal first with the question of residence at courses. If a teacher wants a three month course which is unusual, or which is so highly specialized as to be uneconomic to provide on a large scale, then he must be prepared to go where the course is being run. But for the great majority of courses this would not be the case. It is an unnecessary and unjustifiable interference with the private life of the teacher to be told that if he wishes to go on a three month course he must leave home and go into residence somewhere a long way away. There is no justification for imposing on him the very considerable personal strains that this would involve in his family life. It is no good saying these things are unimportant. Anybody who deals with mature students at college knows that in fact the strains are very real when people have to go and live away from their family, their wives or their husbands. In fact, very many mature students fail on their courses not because of lack of ability, nor because the course is difficult, but because of the personal strains that they impose.

But even if the situation at home can be arranged satisfactorily, it is not right that a teacher should be expected as the price of in-service training to give up his life in the community in which he is working. He may be playing an active part in the political affairs of his locality. Perhaps he is a parish or town councillor. If so, he cannot be expected to drop out of his local political affairs for three months, and not to attend his town council meetings, particularly if he represents a marginal ward or constituency.

Again, he may be secretary of the tennis club, or conductor of the village choir, or possibly one of the two tenors that manage with difficulty to keep the choir together. He cannot be expected simply to withdraw his services for three months. Teachers undertake a whole range of activities which are particularly important in a job where one of the occupational hazards is that you spend your working life surrounded by immature minds. Many of these activities may be of major importance to a teacher as a teacher. Indeed, they may be more important to him than three months' in-service training.

It is wrong that teachers should be expected to interrupt the continuity of these important activities. Consequently if teachers are to be expected to go readily on courses, they should not be asked of necessity to live away from home. Courses must therefore be available within an hour's travelling distance. This sets further constraints upon where they are held. It therefore cannot be assumed that they will be held in colleges of education, for there are many places in this country that are not within an hour's travel of a college of education. It is even less likely that they could all be held in universities. It is not even certain that they could be held in polytechnics, although polytechnics are in general much more accessible to people's places of residence than either universities or colleges of education.

I would like at this point to give a little more careful consideration to the possibilities of part-time courses. The trouble in education, and particularly with regard to higher education, is that there is an underlying assumption that the full-time course is of necessity better than the part-time one. There is also the assumption that if you are planning a part-time course you merely plan separate snippets from a corresponding full-time course. In other words, you spread your full-time course out over one day a week. But there is a case for the part-time course in its own right, designed as a part-time course intimately related with the actual job that is being done in the schools. Indeed, this aspect of the part-time course is already becoming apparent in the Open University. We therefore need not take as read everything that James says about one month or three month courses.

What exactly do I mean by a part-time course? I certainly do not mean a course that is undertaken in the evenings or at weekends, or during the teacher's holidays. A part-time course is not something that can be imposed as an extra in an already overfull professional week. It would still involve release from school. Moreover, it does not mean a day a week. It would probably mean taking a week at a time at fairly frequent intervals. I refer you to one of the few deliberately planned courses of in-service training that deal with organization or pedagogic techniques, namely courses at the further education college at Blagdon in Somerset. They have decided at Blagdon that the most suitable periods for courses of this nature are not shorter than a week and not longer than about three weeks. I am only floating this idea tentatively, but I believe we should look at the question of part-time in-service training as well as the full-time courses envisaged by the James Report.

The next question is who should be responsible for the instruction? To some extent most of us could go along with the James answer. This implies that people who are up to date in their subject shall be responsible for instruction in those courses which deal with subject knowledge, although it is not necessarily true that somebody who is up to date in his subject and spends his time lecturing to undergraduates or full-time adolescent students will be quite as successful with mature students who may have lost the habit of full-time study.

As I see it, a large amount of the instruction, as well as the design and planning of courses, ought to be undertaken by practising teachers. It has always seemed to me to be strange that in all occupations other than teaching it is assumed that progress in the professional skills and techniques will be made by people who are engaged in the job. It is assumed that advances in surgery will be made by practising surgeons, advances in medicine by practising physicians, advances in architecture by practising architects and advances in engineering by practising engineers. But it is certainly not generally assumed that advances in teaching will be made by practising teachers. Moreover, I must regretfully admit that teachers themselves are prominent among those who fail to look to their own professional colleagues for advances in the professional techniques of teaching. If, as I do, you go round the refresher courses organized by the local and county associations of the Union and read the list of lecturers, you will scarcely ever see a practising teacher among them.

I am certain that most of the recent developments in teaching techniques have in fact been made by practising teachers and I would have thought that responsibility for teaching them in in-service training ought to be undertaken very largely by experienced practising teachers. I would have thought that many in-service courses would be in the form of a limited number of lectures combined with study groups, and the discussion of practical situations. If I may refer to the staff college at Blagdon once again, this is a format that they have developed with considerable success. The procedure for a one week course for headteachers on the production of a timetable would be to postulate an imaginary school complete with staff and to ask the students each to make up a timetable. The group would then discuss the various timetables. This technique will undoubtedly be developed to a considerable extent and the implication is that much of the teaching can be and should be undertaken by practising teachers.

What about the cost? I think that James's £20 million was a gross underestimate. Let us first look at the problem of providing supply teachers for the 17,500 who will require to be released from the schools at any one time. This represents 5 per cent of the total teaching force and therefore 5 per cent of the total salary bill, which is at present £700 million. The supply staff will therefore cost £35 million. That is a plain straightforward calculation. Then there is the cost of the building, and I have indicated that in-service training on this scale will require buildings specially provided for the purpose. There is also the cost of the equipment, and the cost of the teaching staff which, if it is to be done by practising teachers, will also lead to a further increase in supply staff. It is only guess work, but if the supply staff costs £35 million, it is reasonable to say that at least another £35 million would be required to meet the cost of the courses and possibly more. It would not be a foolish estimate that the total cost might be as much as £100 million. This is nothing particularly ambitious. It is merely the logical implications of the James recommendations of one term in-service training in seven years. It is worth noting incidentally that the cost of the further education staff college is £100 per student, per week, and this does not cover the cost of replacing the teacher at his own college while he is away on a course.

Now I have thrown out certain suggestions. They are random thoughts rather than positive recommendations. I have suggested that these thoughts flow logically from the James Committee's recommendations. Now I am very conscious of the fact that in the course of what I have said I have built up a major new industry in education. I have suggested a marked increase in the total education bill. I am also conscious of the fact that one of the usual ploys of opponents of education is to indicate that the cost of any advance will be so great that it cannot be undertaken. I am also aware of the fact that another ploy of reactionaries is to discourage the small reforms that are politically possible by emphasizing how much more important are the large reforms that are not politically possible.

In these terms, the sort of thing that I have been talking about could easily appear to be supporting those people who want to pay lip service to in-service education for teachers but who are really quite anxious that nothing much shall be done. Nothing could be further from my intention. In our general criticism of the James Report we should not underestimate the importance of the fact that for the first time an official document has recommended that in-service training of teachers should be deliberately planned on the basis that every teacher should undertake at least one term in seven years. This is a huge step forward.

We are at present at the stage where a good deal of original thinking about what this implies is necessary. One of the risks in setting out on any new development is that the short-term decisions will ultimately stand in the way of the long-term achievement. Up and down the country in all sorts of activities there may be seen instances of procedures and institutions that are hopelessly behind modern achievement because thirty, forty, fifty years ago they were in the vanguard of progress.

Let me give a purely personal illustration of what I mean. My own home town of Guildford required two world wars and the traumatic experience of receiving the evacuated school population of London to convince the town council and the local electorate of the necessity of a public library. Guildford did not have a public library until in 1939 the evacuees from London, having nothing to do, asked 'Where is the public library?'. When they were told there was none they immediately descended on the town council in such numbers that although it was wartime the reactionary town council had to set about providing a library.

But the reason for there being no public library was because in the 1880s Guildford was in the forefront of advance. With the town council's support they had built a working men's institute which had included a lending library, and this institute had gradually gathered to itself a vested interest of respectability and tradition that had subsequently stood in the way of advances that had been easy in other places where they had not been so progressive in the 1880s. You need only look at some of the buildings and school institutions up and down the country to realize that the handicap of progressive developments that time has passed by is the source of very many of our educational problems. Indeed, in the context of industrial development, it lies at the root of many of this country's economic difficulties today.

The final point I want to make is this. We are not likely to see the full implementation of the James Committee's proposals within the next two or three years. It is important at this point in time, therefore, that we do not build up at this stage a number of vested interests and a number of apparently satisfactory institutions which will stand in the way of the ultimate advance when it does come. Much of what has been achieved in education over the past century would have seemed impossible at one stage. When Borough Road Teacher Training Centre first opened its doors to a three month course in teacher training, the possibility of a three year minimum full-time teacher training course would have seemed utterly out of the question. Even as recently as between the wars the BEd degree and the massive volume of higher education now undertaken at the public expense would have seemed beyond the bounds of possibility. The kind of in-service training I have outlined may seem impossibly idealistic but I have not a shred of doubt that at some stage in the future people will look back at the James Committee recommendations and say that it was extraordinary how modest were James's demands.

If for a year or two we have to settle for something less than the James proposals for in-service training, it is important that we do nothing that will compromise their ultimate realization. There is therefore an immense need for the discussion of basic principles and what they imply, so that as we move into a new era we can be sure we start moving along right lines rather than in lines that we shall subsequently regret. The widespread approval that has been given in principle to the James proposals indicates that the time is ripe for a very considerable advance in the field of in-service training for teachers. I would be sad if we directed that potential along the wrong lines.

# 3 In-service training provision: LEAs

## John Taylor

As much of the work of the LEAs is concerned with money and administration, I propose to discuss these topics.

I suppose the one feature of the James Report which has provoked the least disagreement from all quarters is the new deal for the serving teacher—the third cycle. Cynics have suggested that the chronological reversal of the cycles in the writing of the Report was a deliberate attempt to forestall criticism by an early creation of the impression that the Report would prove acceptable as a whole. Coupled with this general approval of the concept of the third cycle has appeared a fairly widespread scepticism as to whether the local authorities, on whose willingness to finance the proposals their fulfilment depends, will in fact be prepared to foot the bill.

I have no doubt that local authorities will wish to look carefully at the financial, and administrative, implications of setting up the proposed in-service training of serving teachers, but I suggest these criticisms are unfair. They overlook the fact that the evidence of all the local authority associations presented to the Committee stressed the importance of expanding in-service training, and they fail to recognize the very considerable developments which the local authorities have themselves initiated over the past seven or eight years. There are, for instance, local authority teachers centres already in existence which do not fall short of the standards of staffing, accommodation and resources laid down for the professional centres in section 2.33 of the Report.

The Report has been widely criticized for not having made an attempt to cost these recommendations, and particularly for not having tried to put a price on the in-service training of both experienced and licensed teachers. I think this is unfair, not only because the Committee were given a very limited time in which to work, but because they left so many options open that any realistic financial estimates must depend on national policy decisions. I have not noticed any enthusiasm on the part of the critics to fill the breach by announcing their own assessment of cost, and I certainly do not propose to do so here, because I realize that there are too many important unknowns to make this possible. The Secretary of State puts the number of additional teachers required at between 15,000 and 20,000, and estimates the extra cost of in-service training as between £25 million and £35 million for teachers' salaries, and £10 million for further facilities; other estimates of the number of additional teachers required are as high as 40,000; one branch of my own association, the Society of Education Officers, has arrived at a total cost of up to £100 million a year for second and third cycle training.

Of the imponderables, I would draw your attention particularly to two. The first is the rating of the licensed teacher. If one accepts the NUT recommendation that licensed teachers should not count against the establishment of the school, then the cost will clearly be very much higher than that required if Sir William Alexander's suggestion that each licensed teacher should be regarded as the equivalent of half a teacher is accepted. We should note Sir William's claim that if his formula is accepted, it will largely offset the additional cost of the third cycle, and note also the fact that many people have reservations about the validity of this claim, reservations which I must say I share.

Again, doubts have been cast on the Report's statement that the number of teachers released at any one time as a result of the operation of the third cycle would exceed 3 per cent, and several commentators have said that the teachers required to replace the teachers enjoying their sabbatical would considerably exceed this proportion.

However, whether you consider the Secretary of State's £35 million or the branch of the Society of Education Officer's £100 million as being the more likely figure, I am not really so much interested in the answer to the question 'how much?' as in the questions 'by whom?' and 'how?' One of the least controversial sentences in the Report is that 'the elaboration of any financial system applying to teacher education and training is beset with complex problems', and before trying to answer these two questions, it may be worthwhile setting out the chief areas of expenditure involved in the Report and the Report's recommendations as to where the money is to be found.

There is the cost of the initial training of the first part of the second cycle, carried out in colleges of education and polytechnics, where students are not necessarily destined to be teachers, and a further complication is introduced by the existence of maintained and voluntary colleges, as well as university departments of education. James assumes that the costs will continue to be shared between the LEAS, the promoters of the voluntary colleges and the UGC.

There is the additional cost of the in-service training of licensed teachers in the second cycle. These teachers are, according to James, employees of the authorities, and I have seen no suggestion that any agency other than the authorities should accept this financial commitment, even from those who believe they should remain on the books of the colleges or institutions where they started their training.

There is the unassessed cost of the suggested national and regional organizational structure: of the National Council, the Regional Councils and the professional centres. The Report recommends that the administration of the NCTETS and RCCDES should be met by direct grant from the DES, but that the local professional centres should be maintained by the LEAS.

It may be surprising that I, as a spokesman for local government, should say that I would prefer to see LEAS accept the burden of financing the whole cost of teacher training, except in the case of the universities, and this is not just because of the merit of simplicity —though I am very conscious of the merit of simplifying public finance as much as possible.

In my exceptions I have omitted the voluntary colleges. I am not sure that the relationship between the voluntary colleges and the DES is as happy as that between the maintainers of the voluntary schools —the LEAS—and those voluntary schools, and I wonder whether this is not the time to take a new look at the position of the voluntary colleges.

The Report itself justifies my belief when it says: 'Decisions about the total level of resources to be committed to the system should be taken by central and by local authorities acting jointly.' This is, in fact, what happens now in every sector of public education. The old tag that our education system is a national system administered locally is translated into financial terms by the practice by which Government allocates resources and the local authorities provide them. I see no reason to vary this practice.

I would like to broaden the base of my argument by bringing in further education. The Report admits that its recommendations will influence education far beyond the boundaries of teacher training, and to me one of the most encouraging aspects of the reception of the Report is the way in which people in further education are eagerly exploring the possibilities of the Dip. HE. My own criticism of the

James Committee is that having made this admission, it has not sufficiently thought of its recommendations in further education terms.

For instance, the Report recognizes the existence of the long established FE regional advisory councils, and recommends that lines of communication should be established with them. It is aware of and seems to support the movement to set up a central agency to 'take decisions about the allocation of total resources for higher education'.

Now the regional advisory councils are nothing if not local authority organizations; the pressure for setting up a central agency has come from the local authority associations, and they see themselves as playing an important part in its functions and accepting the responsibility for financing it. James envisages a parallel two-tier structure dealing mainly, but not entirely, with teacher training, financed by local government. Moreover, the important implications of the James Report for further and higher education mean that there is bound to be considerable overlap; both structures at both levels will, for instance, be very much concerned with the Dip. HE.

Surely, this is a case for rationalization. I believe that there is a strong case for a national/regional organization, but no reason for its being duplicated, particularly as one of the main findings of the Report is that the artificial distinction between teacher training and other forms of higher education is untenable. So I would see a central committee and a number of regional councils whose main concern will be the provision of resources for all forms of higher education. In parenthesis I would say that the willingness of CNAA to undertake the validation of the Dip. HE has made the possibility that this should be done by the regional councils much less likely.

Putting all the pieces together, you will see that the final picture I display is one in which the local authorities are fully responsible for the financing and provision of resources for teacher training in all its stages. And as the Report points out, the support for students taking the Dip. HE and other qualifications will come from the authorities.

One important result of what I have been saying is that a fundamental aspect of political power is the power to provide or withhold resources, and it is a situation with which the local authorities are sufficiently familiar to lead them to expect a greater share in the control of the national and regional councils than the Report's rather naive though flattering proposal that 'each LEA within the RCCDE should have one representative, and here again we would hope for professional representation at senior level, preferably by the CEO himself'. Nevertheless, I believe that experience of the polytechnics has shown that the authorities can exercise their financial controls in an enlightened way, and I see no reason why the various interests which James envisages should not play a real part in policy making, or why professional freedom should be subordinate to financial considerations. It may seem surprising that in answering the question 'by whom?' I have willingly accepted a greater financial load on the local authorities bearing in mind that I am, in Lord James's phrase, 'a natural watchdog of the private purse'. Perhaps my answer to the question 'how?' will supply an explanation.

Tucked away in the Report is the statement that:

> It does not follow that a proper measure of financial control by local authorities is best exercised by the unplanned intervention of individual authorities and the need for better coordinated arrangements is already recognized in the studies undertaken by the Pooling Committee.

Declaring an interest as a result of my membership of the Pooling Committee, I think this is an important recommendation which has not received the attention it deserves. Pooling, as at present operated, has its critics, because it is open to the charge that it can lead to the irresponsible spending of other people's money, but it is possible to introduce controls which can make it a less open-ended financial device. A controlled pooling system has two merits in its application to teacher training: first, it recognizes the fact that in the whole process throughout the three cycles, individual local authorities are financing the national stock of trained teacher activities; second, by acting as an incentive to the smaller authorities, or those with fewer resources, it can encourage the maintenance of national standards. There is certainly a case for the application of a more sophisticated pooling system throughout the range of the three cycles, even including the financial support of students.

In discussing the financing of the James proposals, I have strayed far beyond the limits of the subject of in-service training, but this is because I think it is wrong not to treat the funding of teacher training as a whole. It is very much easier to deal with the part to be played by the local authorities in the administration and organization of the third cycle quite separately.

It might be profitable to consider the situation which will be created in a local education authority whose teaching force after local government reorganization may well be not less than 5,000 or 6,000 by the operation of the proposed third cycle. That teaching force will consist of many different kinds of teachers from schools of different kinds and sizes: teachers in small infant schools, heads of department in large comprehensive schools, specialist teachers of subjects such as Russian or music, teachers of mentally handicapped children, potential heads and careers teachers, to name but a few. Those who are eligible for third cycle training will be faced with a bewildering number of choices from the forbidding list contained in paragraphs 2.6 to 2.20 of the Report. Arrangements will have to be made for the manning of schools while serving teachers in training are absent for periods of from one month to twelve. The Report says: 'The administration . . . of third cycle facilities on the scale suggested here would need to be well-planned and coordinated.' Before I comment on this, I would like to make one point which I consider important. James says that in-service training is a very misleading term, and I would agree. At present it is used to describe two quite different kinds of activity. There is the in-service training which involves the secondment of teachers from the schools, which is held in institutions outside the authorities, taking the form of supplementary courses, degree courses, full-time diploma courses. Normally teachers attend these courses because they want to improve their own qualifications as part of their career pattern. There is no doubt that attendance at these courses benefits the schools and the authorities from which the teachers come; nevertheless, it is generally accepted that the teacher attends the course for his own improvement.

There is also the in-service training which, in the main, is promoted by the local authorities, which is usually made up of shorter periods —week, weekend or day courses and seminars. The last few years have seen an enormous increase in this type of training, so that in terms of student hours it greatly exceeds the first category. Now, although this type of in-service training does bring benefits to the individual teacher, its main purpose is to further the policy—the strategy—of the authority. It may be related to a major change of policy, such as a change from a two-tier to a three-tier organization, to changed circumstances such as an influx of immigrant teachers, to shortages of certain types of teachers, to the introduction of new teaching methods or equipment. In-service training mounted by the authorities is thus normally seen by the authorities as a means of helping it to meet its responsibilities. I believe that the James Report recognizes this important distinction implicitly if not explicitly and

I think that when Lord Boyle talked of courses that teachers want and courses that teachers need, he meant the same thing.

As I read it, the Report sees the coordination of third cycle training as shared between the professional tutors in the schools and the professional centres. I accept that they have a function to perform within the framework of James, although I share the reservation of the NUT about the professional tutors, particularly in the small school, but I believe there is a cog missing—the local authority.

I say this not because the local authority is the paymaster, but because it is an educational entity, responsible for the schools it maintains. It is proper that the school in which a teacher works should, through a professional tutor or some other agency, interest itself in the professional development of its staff; it is also proper that the professional centres should fulfil the purposes which the Report lays down, by becoming 'a forum for the exchange of ideas, information and experience, between new and experienced teachers, teacher-trainers and LEA advisers' and covering 'most of the day to day training requirements of the schools'.

But neither the individual school nor the professional centre is really in a position to assess the needs of the authority as a whole, nor has it the responsibility for implementing the policy of the authority; those things can only be done by the authority itself. The authority must also accept the task of ensuring that the work of the schools is adequately covered during the absence of teachers as a result of the third cycle—a complicated operation, whether it is done by an increased supply staff, an improved staffing ratio or the greater use of part-time or retired teachers. The Report suggests that the authorities' own in-service training programmes should continue on an augmented scale. Only the LEA is in a position to coordinate the two kinds of in-service training.

Moreover, the LEA has the expert staff to undertake this coordination in its inspectorate—and there is good reason to believe that the new authorities created by reorganization will increase the size and the responsibilities of the inspectorate. I am not saying that the individual interests of teachers should not be given full regard, or that the involvement of the professional centres or of teachers should be lessened. There is only one body which is in a position to undertake the programming of third cycle in-service training without breakdown, and that is the local authority after consultation with the professional centres and the schools and teachers. And by programming I mean agreeing which teachers shall be released, the particular form of training they will undertake, and the period of release, arranging that continuity of teaching is maintained and ensuring that a proper balance is achieved between the personal education of the teachers and the needs of the schools and the authority.

I may be accused of upsetting what was intended as a delicately balanced mechanism by a clumsy readjustment of the function of the LEA, or trying to retain for the LEAs a power which they are reluctant to yield. My answer is that the purpose of this book is not to take the Report to pieces destructively, but to see whether its recommendations can be made to work effectively. The third cycle of James presents an exciting prospect, but I do not believe that it can be made to work unless the LEAs are more directly and explicitly involved financially and administratively.

# 4 In-service training provision: colleges of education

## Stanley Hewett

Of necessity this paper will be concerned with the role of colleges of education within an organizational structure which does not yet exist. Therefore, this paper is very much concerned with what ought to or might happen rather than what is happening or will in fact take place.

In addition to this problem, there is no definition of in-service training. Everybody is in favour of it but nobody has clearly indicated what they mean by it. Are we to regard in-service training as any structured educational experience undergone by a teacher in service? Or should we confine the term to educational experiences which are specifically designed to improve the professional expertise and competence of serving teachers? For example, in Bloomsbury, Birbeck College of the University of London and the University of London Institute of Education are close neighbours. A very high percentage of the students at Birkbeck College are serving teachers. The courses they take are not designed to have relevance to their professional careers. Those at the Institute of Education are deliberately designed for such relevance. Nevertheless, it would be difficult to judge which of the two institutions has made the greater contribution over the years to teachers in the Greater London area. There are quite clearly difficulties in distinguishing between the personal and professional education of serving teachers. The Department of Education and Science accepts the difficulty and will permit costs of teachers on degree courses of all kinds to be a charge on the teacher-training pool, the only exception being Open University degree courses. In view of the difficulty of making distinctions I would favour the widest definition of in-service training.

The third problem is that although everybody is in favour of in-service training we should not assume that it is automatically valuable. It is not the universal panacea which the universal cry for it might presuppose. In-service training, particularly where people are seconded on salary, is extremely expensive. We shall not get value for money unless the kinds of in-service training provided meet needs and improve educational practice. The real difficulty is in identifying those needs. Are they the needs of the teachers, the needs of the schools or the needs of the pupils? It would be facile to assume that the needs of all three groups will happily coincide.

Any organizational structure which emerges to meet an expanded provision of in-service training must be capable of identifying and meeting the needs of the education service and the teachers within it. It must also be capable of applying such resources as exist in a rational and economic manner. Such an organizational structure is urgently needed. The very profusion of in-service provision and the variety of providing agencies has given rise to the term 'the in-service jungle'. It is at the moment a rich but somewhat tangled growth, luxuriant in places and proliferating rapidly. The variety is occasion- ally self-defeating. It is, to parody a phrase in the James Report, 'a hubbub of competing agencies'. Such organizational structure as now exists is not well suited to foster and sustain the massive expansion and development which we hope for. Who does what to whom, where it is done and who pays for it are questions which must be answered.

We need an administrative structure which will bring into res- ponsible and genuine partnership all those with a legitimate interest in the in-service training of teachers. These legitimate interests would seem to be the employers, the teachers, the training institutions and central government. The partnership which is created should provide a proper balance of academic and professional interest. Teachers and their employers should meet on equal terms with each other and with the colleges and universities which we hope will be providing the bulk of the activity and establishing its standards.

Administrative structures in the shape of area training organizations already exist. Many would argue that they should continue to be responsible for the coordination of in-service training within their geographical boundaries. While this solution certainly utilizes exist- ing structures, it must be confessed that they may not be well suited to the new and more systematic provision which will be necessary if anything approaching James cycle three is implemented. ATOS vary considerably in size. Their boundaries do not coincide with local authority boundaries. There are also those who would argue that they give prominence to the academic interest and that the professional interests of teachers and LEAS are not sufficiently strongly represented.

As a result many critics have argued for regional administrative bodies rather larger than existing ATOs which could provide a better balance between academic and professional interests and thus produce a more representative partnership. Certainly it would be helpful if regional bodies were of sufficient size to provide a range of in-service provision and if their boundaries did not cut across local authority boundaries. They should also have the power to organize and rationalize provision. It is this lack of authority which is perhaps one of the weaknesses of existing ATOs.

Whatever system of administration is ultimately set up it must as a high priority relate preservice and in-service provision into a continuum of professional education. If they fail to achieve this, professional education will be a series of discontinuous and fragmented experiences in which the preservice and in-service stages are unrelated and the individuals concerned with them isolated from each other.

They should also give urgent attention to the need to rationalize levels of provision into a unified, coherent and progressive structure which would be adapted to the needs of teachers at different stages in their careers. In-service training should provide teachers with opportunities to shape and direct their careers rather more effectively than they now can. In addition to rationalizing levels of provision, an attempt should be made to rationalize the award structure which should accompany it. It would be highly desirable for designated courses to contribute towards some form of ultimate recognition in the shape of defined awards. Defining the levels of courses and establishing the awards that go with them would enable teachers and their employers to recognize professional progress.

The kinds of in-service provision which one might usefully think of would seem to fall into five broad categories or levels. First, all teachers should have easy access to appropriate resources and guidance. They need at all stages in their career what one might term *support services*.

Second, there will be a need for short but concentrated courses on specific and limited topics. These would be a necessity for teachers in the early days of their service in order to remedy the inevitable lacunae in initial training. They would be needed by experienced teachers in order to keep them up to date with a rapidly changing curriculum. Courses of this kind one could perhaps term *specifics*.

Third, there will be a need for higher level courses through the medium of which teachers could have an opportunity to shape their career direction and gain a recognized award. These should be available to teachers after some five years of service to enable them to reflect on their careers hitherto, and to permit them to prepare for future responsibilities. They would serve the function of retrospective interpretation and prospective direction. One might term them *middle management* courses.

Fourth, there will be a need for a relatively small number of people to have the opportunity to prepare themselves through advanced studies for what one might term top management posts in the education service. While advanced courses exist at present, they perhaps do not sufficiently direct themselves to the skills and knowledge which senior executives in educational administration need.

Responsibility for ensuring that adequate provision in the various categories is made should rest with whatever regional or area body is set up. As indicated earlier, its constitution should represent the true partnership of legitimate interests. Clearly local authorities who are responsible for their sections of the education service and who employ teachers should be powerfully represented. They are well placed to assess the needs of their services and of course they must approve expenditure incurred by their teachers. Powerful though their representation should be, it should not be dominant. Teachers should be equally strongly represented together with representatives from the academic bodies, colleges, universities and polytechnics. A dominant position for LEAs could lead to domination of the content of in-service training and compromise the intellectual independence of the professional education which teachers were receiving through this means. Local authorities should not be the sole voice assessing the needs of their employees.

By the same token it would be unfortunate if local authorities through their own inspectorate advisory services and teachers centres became the major provider of in-service activity. There would be a danger that authorities might be tempted to provide only those courses which suited their particular objectives in the running of their educational services. It would be unfortunate in the extreme if control of the curriculum and methods of teaching moved away from the individual schools and the teachers within them. The actual provision itself of in-service courses of all kinds should be remitted to approved agents sanctioned by the regional administration to provide the support, the services and the courses. These approved agents would include professional centres, colleges, universities and polytechnics.

One of the major agents should be colleges of education. They are, and are likely to be in the foreseeable future. major providers of preservice education and training. They are therefore well placed to ensure that continuity of preservice and in-service training which I stressed earlier. The constant contact with serving teachers and the feedback which would result would have extremely beneficial effects upon the kind of provision which colleges made at the preservice stage. It is extremely unfortunate that the colleges' involvement with serving teachers has been so limited hitherto. One wonders why more deliberate efforts were not made to base teachers centres in existing colleges.

Another virtue of the colleges is their wide geographical distribution. There are 157 colleges of education, seven departments of education in polytechnics and twenty-eight university departments of education. While they are not as well distributed in relation to the teaching force as one would wish, they do provide collectively a large number of ready made professional centres. There would be few teachers who did not find themselves within commuting distance of one of them. Apart from the fact that the colleges already have much of the resources, materials, facilities and staff which would be required, they are also well placed to mediate between universities and schools in the field of educational research. Facing as they do both ways they could have a major function as interpreters and entrepreneurs. In the same way they could be agents for the dissemination of curriculum development projects whether initiated by Schools Council or by other agencies. All this is so obvious that it hardly needs saying but one cannot but recall the sharp division between the teachers centres and colleges which exists in very many areas of the country.

The contribution which colleges could make as agents would be in the provision of all but the highest level of courses earlier outlined. Not all colleges, however, could attempt to make provision in all the other categories. Rationalizing according to the need and capacity will have to be undertaken by the appropriate planning body.

All colleges, however, should act as service, resource and support centres for local teachers. In rural areas some means must be found for taking resources to teachers if the teachers cannot easily get access to them. All colleges should act as professional centres for the specific purpose of providing support for teachers in their first year of appointment. Through these professional centres would be established the liaison between the training institutions and the school-based professional tutors. Through this service one would establish the meeting point of preservice and in-service activity. The regular feedback this would occasion would do more to establish proper college/school relationships than any other device. It would also improve the quality of preservice provision by making its providers aware of the needs of young serving teachers.

All colleges could also act as providers for the specific courses needed by teachers in the locality. There would have to be careful rationalization in the provision of such courses by colleges to avoid duplication in some instances and underprovision in others. The content of such specifics should be determined through close consultation between teachers, colleges and authorities.

Some colleges, and rather more than at present, should be agents for and a base for institute of education courses leading to recognized awards. Basing all these courses within the university frequently means that many teachers cannot attend on a part-time basis. Appropriately planned advanced courses bearing in mind regional considerations and utilizing certain colleges as outposts would enable more teachers to pursue extended and high level award-bearing courses than can do so at present, for example, the development of colleges as bases for teaching in-service BEd.

Some colleges should act as bases for nationally planned courses lasting one term or one year. These are likely to be highly specialized courses which it would be uneconomic to consider as regional provision, since they would demand a high level of resources in order to cater for a particular specialism. There is an opportunity for a limited number of colleges to develop as national centres of excellence in particular fields.

Careful consideration should also be given to the use of colleges as centres for short residential courses of the conference variety. Local authorities appear anxious to establish residential centres for field courses, intensive weekend conferences and so on. There is no reason why a college within a particular region or LEA should not devote part of its function to this. Residential accommodation exists and it would be uneconomic to duplicate it elsewhere. Field courses might be widened to include specialist study of urban environments as well as the more rural field centres for geographical and biological work.

The kind of in-service work so far considered has been largely concerned with the kind of activity held to have specific relevance to a teacher's day to day work. There is a strong case for in-service work which is far more subject-centred and concerned with the personal education of teachers. While some colleges might wish to develop such work, it is perhaps more appropriate to think of universities and polytechnics making the major contribution to this particular area.

The task of the colleges is not merely to lay on courses. The real need which they should strive to meet is to pioneer the development of teacher-centred/need-centred in-service education. They must give some hard thought to revising the concept of a course of study for a professional in service. Many existing courses are determined by the needs of the so-called discipline and not by the needs of the teachers. Where this is the case, the courses can appear as Procrustean beds to which those attending are somewhat brutally fitted. Some existing in-service BEd courses are of this take it or leave it variety. We must in future devise study experiences which are built on and intimately related to the teacher's experience as a teacher, his or her professional education up to that point, and his or her professional needs now and in the future. The problem of fostering the professional development of teachers will not be an easy one to solve.

In addition there are other administrative and financial problems to which the regional or area bodies will need to address themselves with some urgency. The planning powers of these administrative bodies must be defined, their finances must give them appropriate independence, they must work out their relationship with the institutions which will act as agents in providing the actual courses. The relationship of regional bodies to any national council for teacher education and training will also have to be carefully examined.

There will also be internal problems which the colleges must solve. They must decide how they wish to staff the in-service activity which they are anxious to undertake. There is a decision in principle to be made. They must decide whether they wish to regard in-service work as additional to the normal work of the college because it is likely to take place during evenings, weekends and parts of vacations, or whether in view of its volume they wish to regard it as part of the normal work of a college of education. In the first instance additional work would have to be paid for by additional payments. In the second case the college would need to be staffed for all its range of activities and teaching in-service work would be expected as part of the normal work of a member of staff. In the latter case the effect on conditions of service would have to be carefully watched. Some uniformity of practice in the solution of this problem is needed if anomalies are not to arise.

The level of staffing required for in-service work would need to be carefully rethought. It is more demanding in time and effort than preservice work. The existing calculations by which one can reckon a number of part-time students equal to a full-time student needs revision. The colleges could not start to work effectively on the existing calculations approved by the DES. The administrative work involved with large numbers of people on a variety of short and long courses is very considerable. If in-service work is mandatory for teachers then reports on progress and other documentation will be also mandatory. The level of work these will produce should not be underestimated.

Colleges and authorities will also have to consider a wider variety of appointments than is now common. Joint appointments which would involve people partly in the college and partly outside the college seem a likely possibility.

Above all some attempt must be made to ensure that the volume and level of in-service work in a particular college remains reasonably constant. No institution can plan its work if there are likely to be marked differences between the load from one academic year to the next. If a college makes provision for a particular set of courses and appoints staff to do them, local authorities must ensure that this provision is fully utilized. To do anything less would be an embarrassment to the institution and an uneconomic use of resources.

I am sorry to end by stressing possible difficulties. While I agree with Lord James that educational ideals should not be always at the mercy of practical problems, one must be aware that these do exist and will become more acute as in-service activity is developed and expanded. I do not think for one moment that they are insoluble, but they will need the sympathetic consideration of those people who must find the money to implement it. Provided that we can identify the true needs and are given the resources to meet them, the development of in-service training in a systematic and structured way would advance the professional education of teachers more than any other single measure. The colleges of education are anxious and willing to play the fullest possible part in this development. It must not become an exercise in making bricks without straw.

48

# 5  In-service training provision: polytechnics

## Eric Robinson

There is no uniform view about the role of the polytechnics at the moment and therefore what follows must to a considerable extent be a personal view.

For a considerable time I have felt that the polytechnics and the further education college sector generally have an important part to play in teacher education, and in fact have been playing an important part for a long time, but this is not a view which is universally acceptable. Whatever view one takes of what is now being done, it could be argued, and I would be inclined to argue, that in some respects the developments in the polytechnics have a significance greater than the numerical scale of things might suggest. In particular, for example, the development of CNAA degrees for teachers, which is not on a very large scale at the moment, has a much greater significance than the numbers might suggest.

I think certain points have been made which have not yet been resolved. There are one or two major questions about the in-service training of teachers on which I would like to make a contribution. I doubt very much that we need an organization for in-service training at all. This discussion does highlight the dangers of overrationalization and overorganization, and it may be that what I want to say about polytechnics and further education colleges in the field of in-service training is that their function in the next five years might be to try and maintain a bit of chaos when everybody else is trying to put things in order. I will try later to make this sound slightly less irresponsible!

The significance of polytechnics and the further education colleges arises from a number of factors. First, their long-standing general involvement in part-time education which had recognized that much in-service education must be part-time. Second, the significance of the development of the CNAA which has hitherto been mainly in the polytechnic sector. Third, the rather curious way in which the polytechnic centres throw up into highlight some of the problems of the

49

present system of finance of further and higher education. In the institution I come from, which teaches education, we get involved with two different sources of finance. We have some education that is financed by one pool, some by another, some that isn't pooled at all and we are under the control of many different bodies : the teacher education bodies, the further education bodies etc. In this sector we can see just how chaotic the state of financing is and what the anomalies are. Finally, the significance of the polytechnic sector is that it is challenging the concept of the universities as the apex of our educational system, which may be of particular significance and importance in the present context.

I want to question an assumption, often implicit in some of our discussions, that we necessarily want an ordered system; and to question in particular the assumption that the isolation of teacher education from the rest of higher education is desirable. It seems that in-service education of teachers will be planned as such and kept separate. I should like to consider whether this is an assumption we want to make, and indeed to ask whether it can be done because one of the first propositions I want to put is that if we attempt to have a closed separate system of in-service education of teachers, a lot of teachers will seek their education outside it and this in fact is the position which is very relevant to the role of the polytechnic and further education colleges at the present time, in the future and in the past.

Looking through the lists of courses and in-service courses for teachers that are officially published by the Department of Education and Science and financed through the teacher-training pool, one finds very little reference to polytechnics and further education colleges and might therefore assume that they are doing little in-service training of teachers. If, on the other hand, a list were made of the number of teachers actually going to formal courses of education in different institutions in this country, it would probably show a majority of them going to further education colleges and polytechnics. The reason behind this is that further education colleges and polytechnics have an overwhelming number of adult students in this country who are entering higher education in evening classes and part-time classes of one sort or another. Most of these courses are not purposely designed for teachers and most of them do not at the moment come within the formula covering in-service training. The courses are of many kinds—academic, practical, long, short, day release, evening and so on. The main characteristic of the courses is that they are established in response to demand from the students—not from employers; they are established informally rather than formally; they are generally outside the orbit of the area training organization. This is all part of the polytechnics' and further education colleges' effort to meet public demand for adult education generally.

Our experience is that teachers demand part-time education, in proportion to their total number, probably more than any other section of the population. A course—a part-time course in virtually anything—can be mounted in a further education college, and a very considerable proportion of the students will be teachers. In particular we found (not only recently but going back for many years) that when we offered part-time degree courses a substantial proportion of our students were teachers. In fact one college that is running a part-time degree course in business studies designed for businessmen has found that a significant number of its students are teachers. So one question I want to raise is to what extent in-service education for teachers should be considered quite separately from post-experience education for the population at large. This is a question which I think has not been raised, but we should examine to what extent the two can be considered together as part of adult education generally. The Open University is quite clearly one example at the moment. The extension of adult education generally will be of value and will be used by teachers. Certainly I would say that whatever happens in the next year or two, the main contribution of the polytechnics and the further education colleges to the in-service education of teachers will be in the continued provision of courses for the general public of which teachers will make a very considerable use.

Another valuable point to be drawn from the experience of polytechnics and further education colleges is that we are concerned with in-service education, not only for private students but also in collaboration with employers, in many fields, and I think it is valuable to look at the provision for teachers in the context of the provision of professional education generally. The problem of the conflicting demands of the employer and the employee and the professional body is a familiar problem for us in many fields. The problem of the student of accountancy, of the professional accountant and the institute of chartered accountants; the problem of the institute of bankers, the bank clerks and the bank managers are all different and I could go through many more examples all of which we are currently dealing with. In the polytechnics and the further education colleges we tend to see the in-service education of teachers simply as one more item in quite a large repertoire. In a number of ways the teacher's education problem is rather an odd one and the provision of education for teachers presents considerably more practical difficulties than the provision of education for anybody else. The familiar problem of further education is that whereas the employers want the students to come so that they will be better in their job, the students generally come so that they can get out of their present job into a better one. So there is an essential difference of approach between employers and employees and anybody providing professional education, and in-service education particularly, has to contend with this. Teaching seems to be a profession in which the employees' interests can be taken into account to a greater extent than most because the teacher's formal working hours are shorter and therefore there is more time available outside their employers' control. I would suggest that there are other reasons than those already advanced in this volume for believing that there are advantages in the teacher pursuing courses on his own account rather than with the permission of his employer. I think we are bound to find as we do in most other trades and professions that some courses are predominantly designed to meet the needs of the employer and will be pursued in working time, but that the employees will still pursue courses for their own purposes, if necessary outside the employers' time. We should seek the valuable reconciliation of these whereby it is understood that to some extent the employee serves his own interest in the employers' time and at the same time serves his employers' interest to some extent in his own time. I have reasons (which I will discuss shortly) for believing that this is particularly difficult in teaching.

We negotiate with employers and employees on courses of many kinds in polytechnics, and in a sense we have to regard ourselves as the broker. If we assume that the system of the future will be controlled either by the employers or by the employees, or by the two working in cooperation, then this puts the polytechnics as a higher education institution in a rather unusual situation. Certainly, in the polytechnics over the last few years we have been very concerned not to become simply the instruments of the employers and we make great efforts to protect our students and protect our curriculum from excessive dominance either by employers or by professional institutions, because in our experience their dominance is not always consistent with the ideals of education that we wish to preserve, and certainly not always consistent with the interests of the employees. I think it is very important that in higher education institutions the provider has a duty to negotiate courses that protect the students from the particular influence of professional bodies or the employers. I have some misgivings about the employers' role in the provision of in-service courses. Under certain circumstances I would prefer some elements of the jungle to continue; and certainly the idea of a rigidly worked out bureaucratic system of in-service education training effectively controlled by the employer is not one which I think any self-respecting higher education institution could view with equanimity. We must certainly cooperate, but when I look at the possibilities, on the one hand of the whole thing being controlled by university institutions, or on the other, the whole thing effectively being controlled by the local authorities or the local authorities and the unions, then one of the reactions, which I and many of my colleagues would share, is that this is not the framework within which we would want to make a big effort. There are other professions which are prepared to offer us a better one and so we would put our effort elsewhere.

For a number of reasons, we in the polytechnics tend to opt for the employee-oriented teaching courses rather than the employer-oriented course under present conditions. The employer influence comes at us in a number of ways: first, there is what I call the ATO monopoly which is generally unacceptable since polytechnics must work in subordination to the university. I think one of the things we can look forward to is that the polytechnics, whatever the government says about James, will not be willing to work under the ATOS under the present structure simply because these are university bodies; second, the very restrictive nature of teacher-training regulations; third, the generally restrictive attitudes of employers and of the teaching profession would not be acceptable to the polytechnics if we get too far over towards the employer-oriented courses. That is to say, we tend probably to run courses to help teachers to get better jobs or get out of the profession rather than to run courses to help teachers to do their jobs better. One of the things we must take into account is the extent to which teachers will use any in-service provision as a means of getting out of the profession unless conditions in the profession are substantially improved. I am sure from my experience that this is one of the motives behind teachers who want to get degrees. They want degrees, not to get better jobs in teaching, but in order to leave the teaching profession.

When we designed a degree course at Enfield some years ago especially for teachers we found that the majority of our students, practising teachers, when asked what they wanted from the degree, replied that they intended to use it to get out of the schools. This was a degree in the sociology of education which resulted mainly in jobs as lecturers in colleges of education.

The teaching profession presents us with more problems in the design of courses than most professions, because it feels it has a certain expertise in teaching, probably quite rightly so. I am a bit doubtful about this: Edward Britton has said that he thought teachers ought to do most of the teaching in in-service courses. I want to stick my neck out and say that I disagree. I am continuously confronted by school teachers who tell me that I mustn't employ people who haven't had some substantial teaching experience in primary schools on teacher training for primary education. I think this can be justified: both primary and secondary school teaching are specialist activities. I happen to think also that higher education teaching is a specialist activity for which most school teachers are not trained and of which they have little experience. And in my experience a school teacher coming into higher education has a very great deal to learn about how to handle adult students and about the skills of curriculum design for higher education and so on. In many respects these are quite unlike school curriculum design and school teaching and I think that it would help us a lot if the teaching profession were able to return some of the respect which I think we give to school teachers, and to recognize that higher education has its own expertise.

But the greatest difficulty is the role conflict of the local education authorities in this sphere. Local education authorities, in my experience, confuse their roles as employers of school teachers and as the controllers of the colleges that train them. In the field of teacher education they claim rights and powers over the curriculum, over the courses and so on, which they would not tolerate were such claims made by another employer. Now in technical colleges and polytechnics we are in a position to see this more clearly. If we had industrial firms or business firms coming along to the polytechnic and making claims to control the curriculum in engineering or in business studies or in accountancy in the way in which a local authority or the Department of Education and Science presumes to control the curriculum in education for teachers, they would be given a very dusty answer. Local authorities are well aware of the need in our field to tell industrial firms that they have rights to be consulted when courses are run that are relevant to their area, but that the curriculum must be firmly in the hand of the academics. However, when we come to teacher education I think that very often the attitudes are different, and I see very great dangers in the sort of role of teacher in-service education that John Taylor proposed, unless the local authorities are meticulously careful to distinguish their roles as customers and as masters of institutions of higher education. This is something which is very difficult for them.

In short, then, I would like to see us making a much bigger contribution to teacher education, but generally I find that the pressures that we come under from various quarters are very much more inhibiting than they are in other fields. We have policies in the polytechnics of developing degree courses for members of the public and developing them in such a way as to meet their needs and very often their professional requirements, and it is a fact that the one area of greatest difficulty is education. Let me just give you one illustration from my experience.

Some years ago I inherited an approval to run a part-time BA degree and I set about planning this course. It was originally conceived as an academic degree in humanities and in order to determine something about the sort of course we ought to run I called in all the people who had made an application in response to an advertisement for this course to come and see me. About fifteen people turned up and every single one was a school teacher. The course was advertised simply as a part-time BA degree in French, English, history—things like this—and every one of the people who found it worthwhile to come to a meeting to discuss the running of this degree turned out to be a school teacher. After discussions we decided that what was best for these people was not simply a BA general degree in various academic subjects, but since they were school teachers and we were an institution committed to running degree courses related to the various career and professional needs of our students, it seemed appropriate that we should have a degree that bore some relationship to education since all our students were practising teachers. We therefore informed the authorities that we would run this BA degree, but we would run it with some relation to education. For a year or two I had very great difficulty with the authorities (these were national authorities) as they said they were quite happy about our running a BA degree, they were quite happy about all the students on it being teachers—this would be marvellous—but we mustn't mention education in this degree because this wasn't our job, this was the job of the colleges of education. It was alright to run an academic degree, but not a degree that had anything to do with education. Eventually I overcame this and then arrangements were made for the Council for National Academic Awards to award BEd degrees and various authorities looked at the scheme that we had proposed and they had to decide whether it was a BA degree or a BEd degree because it had some education in it. And the ruling was if it was to be a BEd degree we couldn't run it because that would be funded from the teacher-training pool which did not include us. But if it was a BA degree then we could run it and eventually it was ruled that one option was a BEd degree which we couldn't run, and the other option was a BA degree which we could run. The extraordinarily curious thing about it was the ruling that was given about the BA degree; the BA degree was the one that included more education studies and the BEd degree was the one that included less education studies. When I queried this I was told that the BEd degrees run in college of education don't have much to do with education. And so we were allowed to proceed with the BA degree specially designed for school teachers; but we were given permission to run it only on the understanding that we nominally made it open to other people so that nobody would be embarrassed because my institution was running a course for school teachers. When we advertised it after being held up for three years we had 250 firm applications within a fortnight.

On a number of occasions I have planned to run sandwich courses both on the science side and the social side designed to have some career outcome through integrated training and so on. In many instances a typical problem is that large numbers of young people coming from the sixth form don't know what they want, but they know and you know that sooner or later they will have to go to work and so the education they have might as well have some bearing on this. One then has the problem of reconciling what they say their interests are and what will afford reasonable career prospects later. We have therefore designed courses with various alternative career options, courses in social science for example with career option in social work, in social administration, in urban planning and in various other fields. The one field in which it has not been possible to develop is teaching because that comes under separate regulations. These are some of the problems that face us and they do not stem entirely from the authorities; there is also a problem within the profession. It is a great pity for example that we cannot attempt sandwich course developments within teacher education, but at the moment these are ruled out by the attitude of the teaching profession as I understand it. These are just some examples to show how teacher education, because of some of the prevailing attitudes, is one of the areas in which although we are meeting very great demands from teachers and from potential teachers, we are generally discouraged from making greater efforts unless we are prepared for very arduous and very tough political negotiations over a long period of time.

What can the polytechnics and the technical colleges do in specific terms? First of all their strengths, I think, are misconceived both by people outside the polytechnics and inside. They are strong in mathematics, science and technology and their staffs in this area include many experienced former school teachers. But polytechnics are not only working in these areas, there is also great expansion in the humanities, the social sciences, social work, business studies, management, art and it is in these areas that I think we should take account of the possible contribution of the polytechnics. In sheer numbers, for example, there are more sociologists employed in polytechnics in the London area than there are in London University and there are signs I think that many of the people in such academic fields are turning their interests to education. Business and management studies are very strongly established in the polytechnics and it may be that one of the best contributions we could make is in teaching some of the management studies which I think are needed by a number of school teachers. We are often criticized because our education departments are segregated. In fact the education departments in the polytechnics up to now have been like little colleges of education within the polytechnic. This was not entirely our responsibility and there are signs now that the isolation of the education department is being eroded. This means that the facilities of the other relevant departments are more likely to be brought to bear on the problems of teacher education and I think there are signs that the departmentalism which often prevents this from happening in the universities is going to be much less rigid in the polytechnics. The sociologists in the education department and the sociologists in the sociology department, for instance, will not be rigidly separated.

I think probably the most spectacular development in the next five years will be the development of part-time degrees under the CNAA and I think a point to make about these in particular is that they are generally purpose-designed for the students that they take, that is they are not simply courses based on a syllabus designed for full-time students which is adapted for part-time students. Generally speaking, the CNAA requires the course to be designed for the people who are to follow it which implies a radical development. We already have the course at Enfield and there is a new course starting at Sunderland Polytechnic for a part-time BEd degree which I think is of considerable interest. The first noticeable characteristic about these degrees is that they will be degrees in education and that in some cases at least there will be no main study element which seems to be almost universal in university degrees up to now. This development will not be limited to the seven polytechnics that have education departments; there are indeed signs that polytechnics are collaborating with colleges of education in their area. There is one polytechnic in the south of England which is putting forward a proposal for a part-time BEd degree to be run jointly with two colleges of education nearby, and I think this may be the first of a number of such cases. I believe that the development of the CNAA part-time degree courses which will be associated with the development of full-time courses under the CNAA will force a break with the ATO unless the ATO relationship can be defined at a different level because it simply is not practical to be working under two academic masters.

Nevertheless, I would hope that polytechnics can collaborate with the ATOS on programmes of in-service training generally. The James Report says that the polytechnics should concentrate on the training of teachers for further education. This is the area in which up to now they have been most strongly discouraged for reasons which I will not go into; but again it is not our fault that we are not working in these areas. I would be, and I think most of my colleagues would be, very strongly opposed to the idea that polytechnics should not continue to develop their interest in education and training including the in-service training of school teachers and certainly this is our intention at North-East London Polytechnic. We are very well disposed to the idea of short courses and in-service courses of many kinds being merely housed in the polytechnic. The concept which Stan Hewett has mentioned of polytechnics becoming support and resource centres for their area is one that very much appeals to us and I think could be particularly important where no effective teachers centres have been established. In the north-east London area we do have strong teachers centres and we have recently had very interesting discussion with the local authorities about the demarcation between the teachers centres and ourselves. The conclusion we have arrived at is that no clear cut demarcation is possible and we have established a standing advisory committee which has representatives of the profession and the local authorities and the polytechnic to govern us on the courses for teachers of preservice and in-service training. We have assumed that we would want to have a continuous discussion of this matter for the foreseeable future. From my experience the lesson learned from industry is that the idea of an employer/employee control of in-service work is an ideal which is very difficult to achieve, and so we are working on the assumption that it won't be achieved. That is to say that for the foreseeable future we will have to act in some respects as an intermediary and we will have to make our own decisions.

We have taken the view that this autonomy is very important and the polytechnic reserves its right to run its own courses, that is to say it must be able to run its own courses even if a local authority or the DES doesn't like them and even if, possibly, the teaching profession doesn't like them either. It is surely an important principle to reserve the right that we offer courses primarily to students and not necessarily to organizations.

The independence of providers is a point I want considered. The contribution of the polytechnics in this field might be of particular significance because of our wider engagement in the problems of in-service education of professional people generally, and in the problem of the provision of part-time education for the general public. I hope we shall not forget that teachers are part of the community at large.

---

The above paper was produced from a transcript of the talk given by Eric Robinson to the Leeds conference. The publishers regret that through an unfortunate misunderstanding they were unable to include a number of amendments which Mr Robinson wished to make at proof stage. We hope that this omission will not detract from the reader's appreciation of the content of the paper.

# 6 In-service training provision: universities

## Geoffrey Mattock

Ever since institutes of education were established, following the McNair report of 1944, some universities have been greatly involved in providing in-service courses for teachers. In fact in some areas during the twenty years (1947–1967) by far the greatest provider of in-service courses has been the institute of education. More recently, i.e. from about 1967 onwards, many universities through their institutes of education have taken initiatives in setting up local committees to coordinate regional activities in the field of in-service training. Because many of the universities have had such a large stake in in-service training for so long, I should like to look back and review some of this work before looking forward to the postJames era.

As providers, the universities offer two distinct kinds of in-service courses: those leading to a 'named award' (i.e. a degree, diploma or certificate) and those which do not. Named award courses can be accurately quantified whereas information about short courses in general is often patchy and therefore incomplete. There are four categories of named award courses:

1  higher degree courses in education
2  first degree courses leading to the BEd
3  special courses of advanced study
4  diploma and certificate courses for teachers of handicapped children

These categories are those given in the DES teachers' course list no. 1.

In 1972–73, twenty-eight universities offered sixty-three higher degree courses. Of these, fourteen led to the award of PhD, eight to MPhil., thirteen to MA, seven to MSc., twenty to MEd and one to MTech. All these lasted for a minimum of one year; some could be taken full-time only, others part-time only and the rest as either full or part-time.

During the same session BEd courses for serving teachers were offered by fourteen universities. It is unfortunate that this particular category of provision is so varied and consequently offers such differing opportunities for teachers in different parts of the country. I feel sure that given a reasonable period of time this situation will have greatly improved and some of the worst anomalies removed.

In 1972–73, 119 special courses of advanced study leading usually to the award of a diploma were offered, and of these ninety were based on universities. The rest, that is about one quarter, were in colleges of education and polytechnics. The general pattern for these courses is either a one year full-time course or a two year part-time course and in some instances they are offered as alternatives.

The fourth category, diploma and certificate courses for teachers of handicapped children, represents forty-two courses of which twenty were offered by universities. As with the special advanced courses they are generally one year full-time or a part-time equivalent.

If we leave out research degrees and BEd degrees this still leaves some twenty-eight universities in England and Wales offering around 160 named award in-service courses of at least one year duration. This would be equivalent to some 500 one-term or 5,000 one-week courses which amounts to a great deal of in-service training.

In-service courses which do not lead to a qualification generally last either for one term or for a very much shorter period. The universities do not in fact offer many one term courses. Of the eighty-four listed for 1972–73, only four are based on universities, the rest being held in colleges of education and polytechnics. However, the universities do offer a very substantial number of short courses of various kinds. Although it is not possible to quantify these on a national basis, some indication of the extent of this provision may be obtained from quoting what is being offered by Leeds University. This session we are offering some 120 in-service courses and conferences which will be attended by well over 5,000 teachers. Some of these events are quite short and last for one day only, but others are relatively substantial and last for three to four weeks. Activity in this field is not static and the present situation results from a gradual build up dating from the founding of the institute. This demonstrates very clearly the fact that the university has positively encouraged the provision of in-service work for teachers. I know that many other universities are also heavily committed to offering a comprehensive programme of short courses for teachers and provide resources for this on a relatively generous scale.

Now most institutes of education run courses both in the university and colleges of education. Almost half of the courses run by the Leeds

Institute are held in colleges. These courses deal predominantly with pedagogical matters and are orientated towards primary or middle school class teachers. But it is the university-based courses which I want to look at more closely. This review of what the universities currently offer is important if the pattern is to change (and I am sure it will) because in attempting to identify the roles of the various institutions we need to see what each has proved that it can do. They fall into the four following broad categories:

1 enrichment courses
2 educational theory courses
3 curriculum courses
4 one-day stands

University staff make a major contribution to the teaching of the first three of these categories. In the case of the fourth the university often serves as the organizer.

The first category—enrichment courses—forms a large part of the programme. In some cases they provide teachers with background material, in other cases they offer teachers an opportunity to update themselves. These courses are given mainly by subject departments in the university and cover topics both on traditional school subjects and increasingly on subjects which are generally not taught in school but which have relevance in one way or another. Particular examples of these subject departments are biophysics, genetics, linguistics, ceramics. This category of courses would generally not be available to teachers if the universities did not provide in-service courses.

The second category—educational theory courses—is largely provided by staff from university schools of education and to some extent competes with courses which are or could be available in colleges of education.

Curriculum courses, the third category, represent a very wide range of courses concerned either with the general curriculum or with specific subject curricula. They are the largest group of short courses offered by the universities and generally include both theory and practice. They are offered at various levels: for headteachers, for heads of departments, for class teachers and for teacher-trainers. They are offered for the experienced teacher and for the less experienced. The majority of courses however include a wide range of teacher status and experience and although this heterogeneity is often most desirable, it sometimes prevents a course from achieving the success it otherwise would.

Over two-thirds of the lecturers and tutors for these curriculum courses as I have labelled them are from the universities; the rest are college tutors, LEA advisory staff or practising teachers.

The fourth category, i.e. the one-day stands, usually cater for large groups of teachers and serve both an inspirational and informative function. They cover conferences on recent research findings, on progress reports of curriculum developments such as Schools Council projects, and other topical issues which are of concern to teachers in schools. To illustrate the kind of activity which goes on in this section here are two examples.

One relates to the dissemination of the findings of a research project and the other to informing teachers about changes which are likely to occur in the field of school examinations. From 1966–71 the Probationary Year Research and Development Project has been working in the University of Bristol School of Education. During the last autumn term, dissemination conferences were arranged in twenty-one universities. Each of these was attended by invited representatives from schools, colleges, LEA advisory staff etc. Setting up these conferences was a particularly interesting exercise, which offered a particularly efficient and economical method of dissemination. The role of the university as the body most able to link up the various agencies concerned with the implications of this project was acknowledged both by those who wished to disseminate their findings and those who wished to learn about them.

My other example to illustrate a distinctive role which the university has to play is the provision this session of six one-day conferences on 'The Common System of Examining at 16 +'. Each of these covered a group of subject specialists and brought together some 150 to 200 teachers at each conference to receive information about the Schools Council Working Paper and the various feasibility studies which are proceeding, but even more important, to express their views about the proposals. Again the university showed itself to be a particularly appropriate institution to draw together the different elements concerned in this matter.

Before leaving the question of university provision of courses, I must mention the way the institutes and schools of education have responded to the advent of ATO/DES courses. These were announced by the Department of Education and Science in November 1969 in order to provide substantial regional courses of duration equivalent to a continuous three to four week course. Funds are made available to ATOS to organize these courses in collaboration with HMI and LEAS. It is noteworthy that these courses are of almost the same length as that recommended by the James Committee as the minimum period for approved in-service courses. An unpublished survey of ATO/DES courses for the financial year 1971–72 by Graham Hammond (1972) of Exeter University shows that sixteen universities organized seventy-four courses. The basic pattern of these courses consists of :

1 an initial full-time period of from two to seven days, usually residential
2 regular part-time meetings over one to two terms
3 a concluding full-time period of one to five days

These courses are providing us with very valuable experience using a new format for in-service courses.

Another in-service involvement of many universities in recent years has been the setting up of science centres. No fewer than thirty-four physics centres, thirty-five chemistry centres and more recently twenty-five biology centres have been established mostly in universities. They were started as a result of initiative taken by the professional bodies such as the Institute of Physics and the Royal Institute of Chemistry and the fact that they have flourished demonstrates both that the university science departments involved have a keen interest in this work and that teachers have found value in attending the centres.

Now I must turn to the future. Clearly it is expected that there is to be a much greater provision of in-service training for teachers. The universities are in a very strong position to make a substantial contribution towards this increase and can and should offer most of the kind of courses which they are currently offering which I have categorized in some detail. I must just add that I do hope that teachers will be able to avail themselves of this additional training which is likely to be provided. I make this point because it is not realized by some people that there is considerable overprovision of courses in some areas and the position is being reached where the various agencies are arranging too many courses for too few teachers, i.e. teachers who are available to attend. I do not propose to say more about this problem; it will suffice to draw attention to the existence of the situation.

Although I have said that the universities must continue to be major providers, clearly there will need to be some change in role because the colleges and LEAs will wish to have an even greater involvement in providing in-service courses than they have at present.

Obviously the university schools of education must continue to offer as many named award courses as are needed. So they must continue to provide higher degrees in education and also the type of courses which are currently labelled special advanced courses although it is likely that many of these will ultimately be converted into degree courses. As there is only likely to be very limited finance available for the development of in-service training, I would not at present wish to see an increase in the number of places available for one year full-time secondments but would wish for more part-time courses to be offered which lead to a named award and also for the development of short courses which could be added together in a credit system to obtain a named award.

The universities must also be concerned with providing short courses which do not lead to a qualification. There is considerable expertise available both in subject departments and in schools of education and this expertise must continue to be utilized both in increasing the knowledge of the teacher and in preparing him in other ways to be professionally more capable. I have already mentioned the kind of courses which the universities can do particularly well and on these they must concentrate. They are the background/enrichment courses, some educational theory courses, although I would also expect the colleges to offer these as well, and finally some of the curriculum courses. In the case of the latter category, the role of the universities might be that of 'training the trainer', i.e. providing professional education for those who might in turn train others. Perhaps the universities should not be much concerned with the very short courses but should instead increase the number of longer courses which they offer.

So much for provision and now to turn to coordination. This is a very difficult issue because each provider wishes to retain its individual autonomy but in my view we definitely need to have good regional coordination. At the least this is an arrangement whereby the individual providers communicate to each other what they intend to offer and thus prevent some of the wasteful duplication which otherwise occurs, and at the most it is a jointly planned regional programme where each provider only runs courses which are approved by the coordinating organization. I cannot see the latter form of coordination ever being achieved nor do I think that it is particularly desirable that it should. I do however believe that if each provider is willing to cooperate in a planning exercise, much can be achieved in using the expertise and resources in a region to best advantage.

Most ATOS have now set up some form of coordinating committees

65

E

and, as one would expect, these have met with varying success. However I do not think that there is any doubt that they have all done a great deal towards promoting improved relationships between the various partners involved.

At Leeds we set up our coordinating committee in 1967 after consultation with the nine CEOs in the area. Prior to this we had an advisory committee on the Institute's programme of lectures and courses. Its membership was nonrepresentative and it did not in practice serve a particularly useful function. Our regional coordinating committee has membership representing each of the LEAS, six of the colleges of education, two teacher representatives, HMI, DES, Schools Council and the other two universities in the area. I should also mention that we have a college liaison committee for in-service training on which one representative serves from each of our fourteen member colleges. This committee is then represented on the main committee by six of its members.

Our regional committee has achieved three things. First, it has greatly improved communications between the membership and we do all now know what courses each of us is offering, what curriculum development groups have been set up and the total provision of in-service training in the region. Second, it has allowed us to understand much better each other's attitudes and problems and third it has encouraged us to be jointly involved in a number of activities. What we have not achieved so far is cooperative planning of the regional in-service programme, but I believe that we shall partially accomplish this in the near future and as I stated earlier, it is probably undesirable to have a coordinating organization which operates a very tight structure.

Some of the other ATOs have also met with considerable satisfaction from the setting up of regional committees and claim that they are working most effectively. Various additional activities are reported to have resulted from the setting up of committees, including surveys of teachers' requirements, publications of pamphlets, evaluation of in-service courses and curriculum development projects. Other ATOs however have experienced considerable difficulties in obtaining co-operation from some of the main providers and there appears to be suspicion that coordination could lead to direction.

I think that one of the very serious difficulties which gets in the way of regional planning is that many LEAS have not established a senior post for the responsibility of in-service training and hence no one, except of course the CEO himself, can speak authoritatively on behalf of the authorities about all aspects of in-service training.

Whilst the chief inspector/senior adviser, if an authority has one, is responsible for the policy of the advisory staff, teachers centres often operate quite separately and without much reference to the advisory staff. Add to this the further complication that finance, release of teachers, grants etc, are usually dealt with by the further education administration and a somewhat complex situation is apparent.

I have quite deliberately avoided direct mention of the ATO versus Regional Council issue. My contention is that the record of many universities as regards provision and regional coordination of in-service training is good, and there I see no need to alter the system drastically. Changes must, of course, come both to deal with a large increase in in-service training which we all expect and also to utilize all available resources as effectively as possible.

These changes might include the involvement of universities which do not at present have an institute of education, so helping to remove the anomalies which cause widespread regional variations in the provision of in-service training.

*References*

HAMMOND, G. (1972) *A Survey of HMI/ATO Courses: 1971–2* Unpublished

# 7 Meeting teachers' needs

## Brian Cane

I have three groups of questions I want to discuss. First, I will take a brief look at the evidence which is available to answer two practical questions:

1 What is the content of in-service teacher education that teachers request?
2 What kind of instructional methods for in-service teacher education do teachers feel they want?

Answers to these questions will be based on the DES/Manchester survey (Townsend 1970) and the NFER Survey (Cane 1969). These surveys were conducted four and a half years ago, but they raise certain issues and points which still apply.

Second, I will discuss two important questions which arise in the organization of the in-service teacher education which teachers feel they need. These questions are:

1 Do we possess an adequate basis of professional knowledge that can be communicated to teachers through in-service teacher education?
2 Have the teachers had an adequate education in the fundamental disciplines which they require to extend their professional knowledge?

Third, I will take a short look at two managerial questions which arise from the first part of my paper, and which must be faced if we are to make progress during the next ten to twenty years. These two questions are:

1 Can we establish effective consultation machinery with teachers on a local and regional basis?

*Table 1 Primary teachers\**

| Topics in order of teacher request | Teacher attendance % | Teacher requests % |
|---|---|---|
| Primary mathematics | 16·7 | 41 |
| Teaching of reading | 2·1 | 30 |
| Infant education | 7·5 | 28 |
| Art and light craft | 5·2 | 25 |
| Junior education | 7·6 | 24 |
| ESN or slow learners | 0·8 | 21 |
| Science for primary schools | 3·9 | 14 |
| School organization/management | 1·7 | 11 |
| Music | 5·8 | 14 |
| Use of audio-visual aids | 1·1 | 10 |
| Environmental studies | 1·7 | 10 |
| English | 4·3 | 9 |
| Religious education | 2·1 | 9 |
| French in primary schools | 3·6 | 9 |
| Physical education | 12·1 | 7 |

*\*Sources*
STATISTICS OF EDUCATION (1970) *Survey of In-service Training for Teachers 1967* London : HMSO   Tables 3 and 23
NB Half the teachers denoted as junior/secondary in Table 3 have been counted here as primary and half as secondary.

*Table 2 Secondary teachers**

| Topics in order of teacher request | Teacher attendance % | Teacher requests % |
|---|---|---|
| Comprehensive education | 2·3 | 24 |
| Use of audio-visual aids | 1·5 | 20 |
| School organization/management | 1·5 | 16 |
| Careers guidance | 1·0 | 14 |
| Counselling of pupils | 0·9 | 13 |
| Programmed learning | 0·2 | 13 |
| Examination techniques | 0·3 | 11 |
| Mathematics for secondary schools | 4·5 | 11 |
| Science for secondary schools | 7·1 | 11 |
| English | 2·3 | 10 |
| Art and craft subjects | 2·3 | 9 |
| Use of TV in schools | 0·1 | 8 |
| ESN and slow learners | 0·7 | 7 |
| History | 1·5 | 7 |
| Geography | 2·0 | 7 |
| Environmental studies | 0·8 | 7 |
| Technical subjects | 2·3 | 7 |

*Sources
STATISTICS OF EDUCATION (1970) *Survey of In-service Training for Teachers 1967* London : HMSO

2 Do we need to modify our concept of the managerial hierachy of teaching, and to break down barriers which seem to separate members of the education service?

Turning to my first two questions, concerning the topics for courses which teachers request. The title for a topic—presented in a questionnaire survey—may not fully indicate to the respondent the content of a course. This may partly explain why few of the general topics presented in the DES/Manchester survey of 1967 were requested by more than 25 per cent of the sampled population of teachers. Nevertheless, it is worth having a look at the results of the DES/Manchester survey since they do provide some evidence on the topics in most demand, and the extent to which these topics were provided in the programmes of 1967. (See pages 69, 70.)

Some of the teacher attendances refer to the same teacher, so that the attendances quoted somewhat overestimate the extent to which teachers attended courses in the topics given.

It is clear that the attendance at courses only partially corresponded to teachers' requests. In particular, it is evident that many primary teachers were either not attending, or were not provided with, courses requested on the teaching of reading, ESN and slow learning children, school organization and management, and the use of audio-visual aids. Many secondary teachers were requesting courses in comprehensive education, the use of audio-visual aids, the use of television in schools, school organization and management, careers guidance and counselling, programmed learning, examination techniques, and slow learners, but they were either not provided with such courses, or they had not attended those that were provided.

I think we might consider the request proportions here as a minimum proportion in view of the difficulty of topic interpretation. However, local organizers can quickly convert the percentages into anticipated attendances. For a teacher population of 1,000 primary teachers and 1,000 secondary teachers, we might expect a minimum attendance of 300 for courses say, on the teaching of reading, 250 for courses on comprehensive education, and about 300 for courses on school organization/management. This would be in a town or county where the general population was about 150,000. We are of course assuming 'convenient circumstances', and this means, I think, no expenses involved, part-time rather than full-time courses and generally, but not always, school time rather than own time, and location within easy travel distance i.e. five to ten miles.

I have stressed that the title of a course may be an inadequate guide when estimating its popularity. It is most important that the nature of a course is properly communicated to the teachers: the treatment of the topic may have to be adequately clarified, and this may dramatically increase attendance. I say this because in the NFER survey conducted in 1967 we found much higher proportions of teachers than in the DES/Manchester Survey who said they were willing to attend the courses we described to them.

The NFER results suggested that the number of primary teachers attending a course say on mathematics, English or reading might double, or even treble, if the course was understood to be dealing with the learning difficulties that any child might have, or with the methods of dealing with these difficulties. Also, we found that these primary teachers would be particularly attracted by courses which were seen to be considering the practical details and aims of recently introduced schemes of work, or which were discussing actual teaching experiences or attending teacher demonstrations. This more favourable response to description of the treatment of a topic rather than just the brief title of a course links with the declared attitude of half the teachers surveyed to the effect that there was a shortage of the kind of in-service education that they might wish to attend, and that the courses that they had attended had had a limited or very little immediate benefit for their teaching.

The secondary teachers in the NFER survey were principally concerned with the operation and application of new apparatus and equipment, and with opportunities to practice with them. They wanted to plan and develop syllabuses in detail so that the content was relevant to the modern child, and arranged in teachable units. They wanted to know about the recent findings of educational research which were relevant to their own area of teaching. Given this kind of in-service course, the participation of secondary teachers in curriculum subject courses might rise well above the 5 to 10 per cent indicated by the DES/Manchester survey and attract the interest of more than 50 per cent of the teachers. I think the point here is that when they see a title of a course, teachers are not always sure what the course will offer: future market research must aim to produce a more detailed blueprint of what is required.

It is interesting that only 14 per cent of primary teachers in the DES survey were interested in school organization, but when we phrased the topic slightly differently in the NFER survey, we had quite a different response: 75 per cent of the primary teachers told us that they would like courses dealing with the pros and cons of new methods of school/class organization, and 66 per cent asked for courses in methods of dealing with large classes of varied abilities with little equipment or space. My NFER report, *The Teacher and Research* (Cane 1968), using a sample in different areas of the country, confirmed this great interest of primary teachers in methods of teaching classes with wide ability ranges, and the interest of all teachers in streaming or setting by ability, and in nonstreaming. That report also underlined again the need teachers feel for more knowledge about methods of diagnosing children's particular learning difficulties, and about methods of assessing children's abilities and attainments. These were precisely the topics which the NFER survey of in-service training found were absent from the course provision made in those counties.

This contrast between the response in the DES and NFER surveys supports the view that it is the professional orientation of in-service courses which is critical. There is a good deal of evidence to show that, given convenient circumstances, teachers will support in-service education which has a strong and relevant classroom orientation.

Turning now to the second of my first two questions, the instructional methods which teachers prefer are related to the kind of course content they desire. In the NFER survey, 75 per cent or more of the teachers said that they would like to join working groups of teachers with the definite objective of exploring subjects or topics in terms of classroom teaching, and which involved participants in practical trials and experimentation with methods, materials and ideas. Almost as many indicated that they would like more opportunities to observe and discuss demonstrations of lessons or teaching activities by other teachers, preferably with classes of pupils similar to their own.

Yet there did not appear to be a wholesale conversion to this approach to in-service education. When asked to select one method for priority, they did not all plump for working groups: in fact between 25 and 44 per cent chose working groups for priority treatment—interestingly, a smaller proportion of secondary than primary teachers, and a smaller proportion in one county compared with another county. The point to stress here is that half the teachers had no single method for priority, or went for the more conventional course methods such as lectures and seminars with discussion and participation. It was obvious that these teachers felt that they had much to learn and receive, and that projects and visits were not the only answers. Perhaps they felt the need for a good deal of fundamental background knowledge that could only be obtained from experts presenting it in a conventional tutorial situation.

The teachers' demand for professional education raises the two questions I posed in the second part of my chapter plan. Are we sure that the professional knowledge, which the teachers want, exists, or has been made articulate? How far can answers be given about comprehensive education, about streaming, about the learning difficulties of children, or about slow learners? Who is really expert about the use of audio-visual aids or of programmed learning? What can we tell teachers about the ways in which they should organize their classrooms for learning? Have there been adequate evaluations of important curriculum developments which we can pass on to teachers?

We have to admit that a surprising number of questions of this kind have negative answers. Further, many have answers which are only partially helpful to the teacher. One quick reply is that there are *some* results from recent development or research projects which are not being communicated effectively but might be, as the NFER report on *The Teacher and Research* showed. Something like two-thirds of the teachers responding to the NFER survey wanted short courses on the most recent findings of educational research in the teacher's area of teaching: few of them were offered such courses.

Yet we must face the grim truth that the present findings of applied educational research—including the evaluation of curriculum developments—are too meagre in many respects to provide an adequate basis for professional decisions. For example, there have been only two large-scale studies of the teacher's day, yet such research is vital to an understanding of the management and organization of school work and the use of resources. Another glaring example is the general absence of the systematic evaluation of teaching procedures and curriculum schemes in specified school circumstances.

There has, of course, been a considerable expansion in expenditure on educational research and development during the last decade from £200,000 in 1961 to £3·1 million in 1971, although the latter figure makes up 0·2 per cent of current educational expenditure. Compared with support for medical research, this expenditure on educational research is very small. The Medical Research Council alone spends £20·6 million a year, and most teaching hospitals have their own research funds which is certainly not true of most colleges of education or university departments of education. Regional hospital boards finance research from their own budgets, whereas only a few local education authorities, notably the ILEA, do likewise. Additionally, the central Department of Health and Social Security spends £5·6 million a year on research relevant to the operation of the health services; one cannot say that the Department of Education and Science spends anything like a comparable sum on the research relevant to the operation of the education service.

I do not think that this is entirely a question of more priority being given to medicine than education, to sick bodies rather than to immature minds. One obvious point is that medical education is more strongly based on fundamental subjects directly related to practice. In this way, the practice of medicine has been made more coherent and intellectually disciplined than the practice of teaching. Dare I say that, apart from its curriculum content, the practice of teaching is still antiintellectual in many ways?

There are two other unpalatable facts we must face: one is that many groups of teachers have not, as a rule, effectively shared their expertise, or systematized their collective experience in a coherent way. Only with the recent growth of curriculum development have we begun to communicate through specialized journals, or through local project meetings. Teachers have worked for too long in isolation. The second fact is that generally teachers have not been keen to support the research and investigation which might expand their professional wisdom: there are many reasons for this, and the climate of opinion has been changing recently, but the official teacher unions and associations have not been very vocal in support of a policy of more local and national research.

This situation also reflects the fact that the professional education of teachers—as distinct from their higher education in traditional academic subjects—has not been sufficiently demanding in the intellectual sense. More than half our nongraduate teachers today have only two years of preservice training, and the remaining three year trained nongraduates followed a course in which at least half of the additional third year course was given over to traditional academic subjects. In all these courses, as in postgraduate certificate courses, the study of education has often left much to be desired, and professional studies proper (i.e. applied education) have been a hit and miss affair in many institutions, and in many LEA programmes of in-service education.

Gradually we are taking this situation in hand. We now insist on three or four years of preservice education as distinct from the two years we accepted only twelve years ago. In terms of quality, we are rapidly moving towards an all graduate profession—indeed in some localities much more rapidly than is generally realized. At my college, we are sending some 420 trained teachers into the schools each year. Of these 420 teachers, 220 are graduates and only 200 are nongraduates. Nearly half the graduates hold BEd honours degrees of the University of Sheffield. This kind of distribution between graduates and nongraduates is becoming commonplace in many of the larger colleges of education.

But what kind of graduate do we need? Are all degree programmes appropriate for a profession that needs to think out, challenge and communicate its own working principles? In short, should we now be questioning the first degree education of our teachers, not just in terms of the James considerations of the probationary year and the issues of consecutive or concurrent training, but also in terms of the content of the course? This is very relevant to any discussion of in-service education that meets the needs of teachers. I believe we have to consider whether our teachers have a sufficiently sound grounding in the fundamental disciplines such as child development, social psychology, psychometrics, sociology, philosophy, comparative study of educational institutions, management and organizational theory, elementary research methods. Without such a basis, which many practising teachers just have not got today, it is difficult to see how we can build on the required in-service education and research that is needed and that is something much more than tips for teachers.

A reorientation becomes particularly important when considering a BEd degree for serving teachers. We know from the DES and NFER surveys of 1967 that BEd courses were asked for by one quarter of the teaching profession, and excluding heads, by something like one third of the assistant teachers. We also know that most of these teachers would like school-based in-service work. It would be logical therefore to consider an in-service first degree which was based purely in professional subjects, and related to the teachers' own experience. We are beginning to see attempts by some universities to introduce such a degree.

The Open University is producing some very relevant unit courses, but its programmes must inevitably lack the focus of local involvement and courses directly related to the teachers' own circumstances. Apart from Lancaster, several universities are discussing part-time BEd degrees of a new type, breaking away from the established BEd pattern for a fourth year course in education combined with a course in a traditional academic subject. This idea is to make a double education syllabus with a professional bias.

The new BEd pattern might start with a problem arising from the teacher's school experience and develop this into a study of the curriculum of the primary, middle or secondary school, with a special study of the content area of a subject of the school curriculum, or of some chosen school problem such as counselling, school management, or language development. Studies of the fundamental educational disciplines would then be studied as ancillary courses to this programme. An alternative pattern might reverse this order, and start with a thorough grounding in the basic disciplines required, and lead on into curriculum studies or specific areas of school operation. If these new type BED programmes could be offered to teachers on a suitable regional basis—either as a three year part-time course, or as a one year full-time course preceded by one year part-time— then the 1967 surveys suggest that the courses would certainly be viable in terms of recruitment, leading to a desired expansion in the intellectual basis for teaching practice.

Now I come to my third group of two questions concerned with consultation and the management of teaching. We have seen that the great majority of teachers are keen to support an in-service and research programme which has a professional orientation and is related to their school circumstances. They recognize their need for more professional knowledge, and many are willing to participate in research which will extend that knowledge: quite a few feel that research is itself a potent form of in-service education—as one teacher said: 'Research can make you think; this is the important thing, make you think more about your job and what you are trying to achieve.'

Yet teachers recognize that they cannot organize their own in-service work or conduct research *and* teach a normal programme in school. Part-time release or secondment for short periods is seen as one answer: the appointment of teacher-advisers, teacher-organizers, teacher-tutors and teacher-researchers another. Whilst appreciating the need for full-time appointments of this kind, teachers want training and research to be in some sense locally based and locally relevant, so that they have a chance to stress their own circumstances and to name their own reservations, suspicions and feelings. There is a paradox in the situation—training and research programmes must retain close contact with the classroom, but these programmes cannot be effectively organized except by full-time persons with time to think and plan, and who then—by definition—will no longer be teaching in the classroom.

There is no doubt that a majority of teachers consider that they are seldom consulted about in-service education, and that such consultation machinery as exists is ineffective. Teaching is a job often practised in isolation from colleagues, and many teachers feel detached from the centres of power and decision. For many classroom teachers and heads, the in-service education that is provided has little reference to the hard practical realities of teaching. Their attitude may be a traditional reaction to authority and to particular local arrangements; certainly I found that the proportion of teachers complaining of lack of consultation varied considerably between three counties surveyed. Obviously, consultation about in-service education is linked with consultation about many other professional matters, such as reorganization, design of buildings, research projects, staffing etc. It does not take an expert in management science to appreciate the effects which defects in consultation and communication may have on the morale and effectiveness of teachers.

What are the practical difficulties? Clearly, the problem varies in intensity from the small, compact county borough to the large rural county or the sprawling industrial city. At the school end, there is a distinction to be made between the smaller number of comparatively large secondary schools, and the much greater number of dispersed small primary schools. There are functional problems such as those of advisers or teacher trainers whose visits to schools are limited by all the other work they have to do. The enemy of everyone—teachers, heads and others in the education service—is that of time—time to give the minimum of consultation and communication with colleagues that is required.

Turning from the sensitive spots, what are the practical possibilities for consultation? Talks between officers of teacher unions or associations and LEA education officers will be only exploratory and informational even though such talks will be valuable especially in the initial stages of some scheme. Perhaps the role of the associations is to clarify procedures and act as watchdogs. The real consultation must be with the whole body of teachers.

LEA advisers, organizers or inspectors will visit schools and classrooms and can make the personal contacts required, but their contacts may be too few and too infrequent. The job of adviser includes appointment of staff, advice on buildings, helping probationary teachers, apart from the organization and administration of in-service courses. There is little time for consultation, discussion or research, especially when the average county will have only one adviser to 300 or 350 teachers. One adviser in a rural county told me that it had taken him two years to travel round the primary schools in his area and have meetings of primary teachers to discuss development of religious education in the schools.

An alternative is to ask heads or senior teachers to a central meeting at which these representatives of teachers express views or receive information. Both small and large authorities organize meetings of this kind, sometimes several a year. This may be a useful communication channel, but the large public meeting is never wholly successful in this respect, and cannot substitute for contact at school level, especially with assistant staff. Further, the feedback is dependent on individual heads.

Lastly, there is the questionnaire survey to every teacher, a kind of market research by post. This certainly has a place, and may be invaluable provided certain conditions are fulfilled. The questionnaire must be most carefully prepared and subjected to a pilot survey with thorough analysis. Voluntary groups of teachers can be most helpful in this task, as I found for the NFER survey. Before we went to the three counties, the Surrey Educational Research Association helped me conduct a pilot survey with 1,000 teachers in Surrey. Another condition is that all the teachers must understand the purpose of the survey and the way in which it has been prepared and conducted. Also, the future use to which the authority intends to put the results. Only in this way will teachers have sufficient confidence in the survey to respond honestly and willingly.

Of course we really need a combination of all these approaches. There is an urgent need to expand the advisory service very considerably. This is one of the major challenges to local authorities in the postJames period. Many parts of the curriculum are not covered by specialist advisers: in 1967, only eight counties had an inspector, adviser or organizer for mathematics, ten for science, eight for modern languages, two for religious education and six for audio-visual aids and television. There should be sufficient advisers to cover all curriculum aspects as well as the administrative tasks. In the expansion of this service, we need to consider how the service can be more locally based and how the expertise of senior teachers and of teacher trainers can be utilized.

We really need to take a cool hard look at how we are using all the local and regional resources of senior staffing and material resources. This management study will inevitably consider how best to group schools for in-service education, curriculum development and research. It does not follow that the best unit for purely administrative functions is also the best unit for this purpose. The unit needed must be small enough to allow the associated advisers and senior teachers to move around and know the teaching staffs. Within the unit, senior teachers would possibly work in several schools instead of one. A college tutor would be assigned to one unit of schools, and would be thought of as part of the staffing of these schools doing a specialized job, not as someone from another planet.

Summarizing, what I am saying is that consultation requires that we rationalize the jungle of educational management which exists between the classroom teacher, and the administrative headquarters where finance, buildings grants and committees form the necessary activity. At present, this jungle is occupied by heads of school departments, heads, advisers, researchers, teacher trainers, and education officers when not engaged in formal administrative work. The rationalization requires that we rethink the staffing unit in local systems of education: schools, colleges and education offices must reconsider their independence and isolation. A rationalization of this kind would go a long way towards meeting teachers' needs for in-service education and professional advance.

*References*

CANE, B. (1969) *In-service Training: A Study of Teachers' Views and Preferences* 1967 Slough: NFER

CANE, B. and SCHROEDER, C. (1970) *The Teacher and Research* Slough: NFER

TOWNSEND, H. (1970) *DES Survey of In-service Training for Teachers, 1967* London: HMSO

# 8 The role of the school in in-service training

## Roger Watkins

In the current reappraisal which in-service education is receiving the school is perhaps the most neglected factor in the whole process. (The term 'in-service education' is, it is felt, perhaps preferable to the more usual 'in-service training'. The concept of training is less appropriate to the further professional development of teachers than the more open and flexible idea of education.) Two substantial research projects in this country have concentrated on the providers of in-service courses and the teachers who attend them and we have a reasonable amount of information on the range of courses available, the kinds of subjects which interest teachers and the administrative arrangements which are most likely to attract them to the courses. We know little however about the impact of in-service education upon the professional development of a teacher or the capability of a school. We know next to nothing about how successful teachers are in relating the generalized experience of in-service education to the particular situation of the school in which they teach. We are ignorant about whether or how schools plan to use the knowledge and skills gained from the attendance of members of staff on courses. However it is the argument of this paper based on experience, observation and what little research data we have, that an understanding of the complex relationship between in-service education and the schools is essential if the maximum benefit is to be obtained from the programmes of further professional development now being organized on an expanding scale.

These programmes may be divided into two broad and overlapping categories. First, those courses which have implications mainly for the development of the individual teacher's skill and resources and which do not involve directly any other teacher or the general policy of the school; second, those courses which imply decision-making involving more than one teacher and which may have major implications for the policy of the school as a whole. In more detail, the first category includes courses which add an item to a teacher's repertoire normally supplied in initial training but which for one reason or another is still missing. A teacher might attend a course on puppetry because he sees a use for this skill in helping his pupils to acquire greater facility with language. Also within this category come 'conversion' courses which enable a teacher to change a career direction. An interest in the personal welfare and interests of young people developing, for instance, from close association in the craft room or on the games field might encourage a teacher to explore aspects of vocational guidance or counselling and perhaps to devote all his energies to this, instead of to his former 'subject'. An in-service course would be the logical next step. Similarly courses which bring teachers up to date in a subject or which extend an area of knowledge do not usually have a major impact on colleagues who do not share the same interests.

In the second category however there is a different situation. Here we include all those courses whose content cannot be applied to an individual teaching situation defined only by one teacher. Courses on integrated studies, mixed ability teaching and compensatory education, for example, must be shared if they are to be effective. Moreover there is evidence to suggest that there is an increasing number of courses of this type which raise fundamental questions of school policy but which will remain inert unless their implications are considered by the staff of a school as a whole and not merely by an individual teacher on his own.

From the oversimplified account above of the spectrum of in-service education courses it will become clear that in-service education is inevitably entangled with personal change and with curriculum innovation. The school has an important supportive role to play in the first and a crucial defining role in the second. (By school I refer mainly to the total teaching staff of a school charged with the major pedagogic responsibilities of the institution but do not wish to imply that the pupil body or the nonacademic staff are not part of the school. They are crucially important since, among other things, they define the area of manoeuvre for pedagogic decision-making.) If personal professional change and development are to be achieved with the minimum of distress to all concerned then the individual teacher needs to feel that he is a member of a liberal and flexible institution which regards such change as a natural and fully understandable response to the challenges of the profession. We can no longer expect the period of initial training to equip a new member of the profession for all he is likely to encounter in the rapidly changing educational scene. Schools must encourage adaptability and a willingness to retrain. There is still an unfortunate tendency amongst some teachers to regard those who attend in-service education courses as merely promotion chasers. Promotion is of course a perfectly proper incentive to professional development; the mistake is to see attendance on in-service courses *only* as investment in career progress and not as a response to a particular professional need. It could be that one of the reasons why some regard in-service education in this light is because they feel it has manifestly failed to engage with real problems experienced at 'the coalface' of teaching. This has undoubtedly been the case in the recent past and many in-service tutors and organizers are currently working to make courses more effective and useful. However it often appears that teachers attending courses do not expect to be able to employ the lessons learned to their immediate teaching situation, because the school (colleagues as well as head) do not welcome the changes envisaged. As Perry (1969) has argued, some schools assume that teaching is a stable and routinized skill which can be acquired through regular confrontation with a large number of practical situations. In this way teaching is seen like carpentry to be learned while doing. These assumptions act like a negative 'training' on the new teacher:

> This sort of training does not envisage the situation for which the new teacher is being trained as a changing one but a static one. And the training is particularly adjusted to the production of teachers conforming to the version of the traditional view currently held in the particular school about the work of a teacher.

It is perhaps worth stating here that it is not suggested for a moment that in-service courses are above criticism. In-service education has clearly suffered from the neglect shown it in recent years by researchers and educationists generally. There is undoubtedly a great deal of irrelevant and idealistic nonsense masquerading as professional development and there is also much to be learned about the art of mediating to teachers the results of educational research in such a way that it makes a vital connection with the stuff of teaching, that it illuminates the genuine problems which teachers might bring to an in-service course.

Roe (1971), writing about the refusal of many teachers to consider the conclusions of educational research, quotes one teacher's complaint as typical:

> This is why it is all so useless. The research is done in laboratories and sometimes classrooms in other places; the findings belong only to those other places and in any case they are never definite enough but simply tell you this was significantly (which in practice means 'slightly') better than that or that the chances of something happening are rather better than even. My classroom is another classroom, my students are other students, I am another teacher. We really almost all the time have to get our own solutions to teaching and learning problems.

This rejection may have two possible causes. First the necessary objectivity of research in education may not seem to match with the essential subjectivity of teaching. Second there is a two way failure of communication; neither the researcher nor the teacher has understood the problem of the other. In-service education tutors should strive to bridge this theory/practice gap and become aware of their involvement in communication as Roe concludes:

> I believe that these gaps in communication among people involved in education have some far-reaching implications. . . . This is not just a matter of interest in subject-matter though that is obviously important. Nor is it just a matter of intelligibility—whether the vocabulary or the syntax is difficult, the ideas unfamiliar. We respond to the *style* of the communication, which may include subject-matter, syntax and the rest, but also the attitudes and assumptions of the speaker or writer, his approach or methodology, his theoretical orientation.

To be successful in-service tutors need to establish a dialogue between the constructive objections of the experienced teacher and the theoretical argument of educational reformers. At the same time they will recognize that the process of personal change can be a disturbing experience when teachers are called upon perhaps to discard a set of perspectives and skills which provide a professional identity. The school's support at this time in providing a framework in which retraining is normal and moreover in supplying the wherewithal with which it can be realized is vital. An art teacher who is denied both the encouragement to add simple film-making to his repertoire and any money for film to put in his own camera which he is prepared to lend to the school will naturally feel frustrated. While a year tutor who develops a real skill with vocational counselling but is denied any time with which to practice it might reasonably but reluctantly regard the in-service courses he attended as wasted as long as he remains in his present post.

It is already beginning to prove difficult to distinguish the two categories of courses outlined above inasmuch as personal change in teachers so often touches upon issues outside the individual. The school as a factor in in-service education looms even larger when in-service courses are concerned from the outset with matters of fundamental educational policy. Schools sometimes complain that they are buffeted from all directions by the winds of change and are seldom given a decisive sense of direction. It is the argument of this paper that schools need to develop a considered plan for innovation and a corresponding strategy for the in-service education of appropriate staff. Two points need to be made here by way of clarification. A plan for innovation does not imply an uncritical acceptance of it. It means a willingness to be open to the need for change but implies also a systematic approach which does not commit the school to inappropriate innovation or more than the school can digest at any one time. It also must be emphasized that a school's strategy for in-service education is not intended as a constraint on the right of any teacher to pursue his career by choosing to take any in-service course. The strategy should be seen as a plan to ensure that training is given to those who are going to implement the innovation goals of the school.

Who will devise the plan for innovation? In the English education system it is clearly expected that this will be the headteacher. Traditionally the head is looked to by staff and outside agencies alike to provide the inspiration and direction for policy-making. His attitude to professional development is therefore crucial. The head who has the confidence of his staff can create a climate in which colleagues can undertake in-service education with some guarantee that the personal and institutional implications of those courses will be at least considered sympathetically. Rubin (1969) concluded that 'In-service education is virtually useless if the objectives of the training programme are not valued and rewarded—if with nothing more than esteem by the power structure of the school.'

There is a problem here however. Whilst it is true that upon a headteacher's sensitivity to changes in society in general and in education in particular will depend to a large extent whether his staff will be able to grow professionally to the benefit of themselves and the school in which they work, it is also true that because of the pressure of the immediate and diverse problems which beset such increasingly complex institutions as our larger schools, head-teachers have great difficulty keeping in touch with these changes. In order not to place excessive burdens upon colleagues already overworked a head sometimes has to miss valuable opportunities to keep himself up to date. It will be as well for both heads and providers of in-service education to realize this fundamental hindrance to professional development not only of the headteacher but also of his colleagues. Regular release for headteachers to update themselves in educational developments is an obvious necessity and perhaps as an interim and supporting measure an information service might be organized providing abstracts not merely of educational research in learned journals but development on all aspects of education from curriculum development to interaction analysis and from community service to educational technology. Heads themselves set great importance upon visits to other schools where experiments are being tried and innovations are being introduced. It would be helpful if an agency could be established through which applications to visit might be filtered. Such an agency would assist heads who wished to find out where interesting developments were taking place and protect schools from excessive haphazard visiting and the concomitant administrative load.

To this point it has been assumed that the headteacher has been directly responsible for the professional growth of his staff. What happens when, as the James Report suggests, this responsibility is delegated in large schools to a 'professional tutor'? It remains to be seen whether the authority of the head in English education is such that such a 'hiving off' of traditional responsibilities can be achieved. Certainly the professional associations while admitting the need for a more systematic and comprehensive care of probationers have set their faces against a more elaborate role for professional tutors. Some American experience is relevant here. Describing some research he directed in in-service education, Rubin (1969) concluded:

It was our belief that a school-centred approach to professional growth would necessitate an on-site agent, someone able to manage the programme of self-developments. Moreover, we felt, on the basis of previous work, that the school principal could not serve this function. The need to achieve stability amidst change normally presents the building administrator with a difficult role conflict. Moreover, experience has led us to suspect that one person cannot proficiently serve as the *permanent* changemaster in a school. Consequently, in our study, a teacher selected by his faculty colleagues and given special leadership training, was used as the training agent. The results were extremely impressive—so much so, in fact, that we now conjecture that *a practising teacher is the best possible trainer of teachers.*

For want of a better name we chose to call these teacher-leaders, facilitators. They provided us with some of our most striking successes. Their value was heavily endorsed both by the teachers and the principals. All participants in the experiment seemed to agree that a teacher-facilitator, freed from teaching responsibilities for a part of the day, is a potent asset to a staff's professional growth.

There is surely room in English education for a limited experiment along these lines (if indeed is it not already being tried) and one looks forward to learning of its success.

It is evident however that a 'changemaster' cannot work without a policy. What is being suggested is that a school should select from all the opportunities for development currently on offer those which seem most appropriate to its goals and its resources. Staff members will then be encouraged and assisted to join appropriate in-service education courses wherever they are available so that the policy may be implemented. The school has no need to regard itself as the mere recipient of training. It should take an active part in ensuring that in-service education to meet its declared needs is made available regionally. Most organizers would be delighted to respond to clear guidance on what schools need and want. When that training has been received, the school needs to make clearly defined arrangements for extending its benefits to all members. Ideally it might be arranged for a group of teachers from the same school rather than individuals to be trained. When a group within the same school latches on to the philosophy of an innovation there is a greater likelihood that it will be profitably sustained. There are a number of possibilities here. A group within the staff might be identified, or might identify themselves, to receive training. The group might be a subject department (for example, deciding to adopt an audio-visual method of teaching a foreign language) or it might be a group with common interests (for example, year or house tutors who wish to find out more about the skills of counselling). If it is unrealistic to imagine that the whole group could obtain release or make arrangements, or perhaps even be willing, to all attend at the same time a course provided by an outside agency, then a means whereby the essentials of the course can be communicated to those unable to attend needs to be devised. Departmental meetings, circulated reports and demonstrations are all time-consuming but vital parts of the in-service process.

The next step in professional development is school-based in-service courses. By this is meant courses which are arranged internally by a school for the training of its own staff members. School-based courses have the advantage of bringing together for discussion those who are going to work together on a particular problem once the course is over. The traditional course drawing on teachers from widely different experience and geographical background spends a great deal of time on the inevitable rituals of social interaction practised by a group of professionals coming together for the first time. Teachers often say that they are just about ready to start on their discussions as the course draws to an end! Furthermore school-based courses can be most closely tailored to local needs and resources. Ron Pepper (1972), the headmaster of that ill-used London comprehensive, Thomas Calton School, has described the way in which the staff organized themselves to move into the new school originally promised them but later refused by Mrs Thatcher. Pepper argues that:

> School-based in-service training sessions learning within one's own teaching environment would do much to help encourage more teachers—and more heads—to adopt a more positive attitude to regearing and revitalizing teaching techniques.

Thomas Calton staff established their policy of priorities, which included training in the use of audio-visual equipment and the development of team teaching and integrated studies, and developed an internal programme of training. Pepper concludes that:

> The mere act of working together has itself been a training process, one which promises invaluable returns as our work and experience develop. One other aspect of this 'self-training' programme has been the way in which individuals have become aware of the gaps in their own past training and experience; whilst having to comb through the school library, assess and cost the equipment and materials required and list and catalogue what resources we have built up has been exhausting but worthwhile.

This is a persuasive but demanding model and a less ambitious start to self-training might be considered. A staff conference is now by no means a rare occurrence but still perhaps not adequately exploited. An example of what might be done will perhaps make the possibilities clearer. Let us imagine that a head and his staff are dissatisfied with their present piecemeal arrangements for pastoral care and vocational guidance within the school. One or two members of staff have attended courses including a one-year diploma course on school counselling. This whole area has implications for every teacher in the school. The in-service courses attended by individuals cannot bear fruit unless colleagues are given a chance to consider those implications. A head might therefore seek the permission of the LEA to close the school for a day in order to arrange a forum on this topic when discussion might be opened by two or three visiting speakers supplemented by the members of staff of the school with special interest and some training in this area who would take the opportunity to relate what outside speakers say to the particular situation of the school. Group discussion might follow on the day itself or be arranged by these teachers as a followup. The aim could be either to implement a policy decision taken by the head or to pave the way for informed decision to be taken on a policy for vocational guidance by all those who are involved in policy-making in any particular school.

Visiting speakers, expert in their own field, are however expensive. Three such lecturers might cost together with travelling expenses at least £60. It is unlikely that many schools could spend this amount from unofficial funds without curtailing other activities. A case might be made to the LEA however that such expenditure (which might easily be exceeded by the expenses of individual teachers from that school attending in-service education courses in any one term) might justify a special grant on the grounds that the money is more likely to provide a good educational return when used in this concentrated way than when used on individual and isolated in-service experiences. Conferences of this nature might well be mounted in cooperation with traditional agencies for in-service education who could focus their administrative services in assisting perhaps as many teachers in one school as they normally do from a variety of schools on the orthodox course. Teachers centres have a useful contribution to make also. Probably too many teachers at present are sceptical of their value because they are not prepared to make centres work for them. The directors of centres could be instrumental in arranging and assisting school-based in-service education by offering advice and facilities and might also arrange visits and exchanges between local schools.

Nothing in this paper is intended to threaten the existing provision of in-service education. The services offered by LEAS, DES and ATOS should be strengthened by the suggestions made that schools should participate more actively in the training process. We are after all concerned with *professional* development and this, to be successful, requires the participation of the profession. As in-service education becomes less of a privilege and more of a right, teachers will demand that it be of high quality and tutors will want their courses to make a significant impact not only upon the careers of those who experience them but upon the schools where they work.

*References*

PEPPER, R. (1972) In-service training and the Thomas Calton School, Peckham *Forum* 14, 2

PERRY, L. R. (1969) Training *Education for Teachers* 79

ROE, E. (1971) *Some Dilemmas of Teaching* Melbourne: OUP

RUBIN, L. J. (1969) *A Study of Teacher Retraining* University of California: Centre for Coordinated Education

# 9 Strategies of curriculum change

## Eric Hoyle

The purpose of this paper is to outline the major strategies of curriculum change which have been in play in recent years, and to relate these to the in-service training needs of teachers. The argument of the paper is based upon three propositions. The first is that effective curriculum change involves concomitant changes in the educational values held by teachers, in the pattern of working relationships amongst teachers, and in the internal organization of the school. The second is that, without denying the crucial role of the creative and imaginative teacher, or of the headteacher whose charisma can generate radical change, innovation for the most part needs to be carefully managed. And the third is that it is currently necessary to develop new patterns of in-service training to support the management of change.

Throughout the paper the term *curriculum change* is used in its broadest sense to embrace change in methods, materials, hardware, school organization and educational principles; that is, virtually any sort of innovation at the school level. The school is treated as the focus of interest throughout, partly because time does not permit any consideration of change processes at other levels of the system, and partly because it is the argument of this paper that the school is the most significant innovating unit.

The discussion falls into four major parts. First, three major patterns of curriculum change in recent years will be outlined. The second section will consider the problems associated with these patterns at the school level. The third section will consider an alternative strategy which could possibly overcome the shortcomings of the three discussed. And, finally, some implications of the fourth strategy for the in-service training of teachers will be considered. Before starting, however, it is perhaps necessary to anticipate to some degree objections to the way in which the argument is presented. Although the paper is naturally focussed upon change, the point must be made that change in education is not necessarily always for the better, especially where the changes are 'promiscuous' and the outcome of thoughtless bandwagon leaping. The paper is organized around a number of summary concepts which conceal the complexities of the real world of the school and the classroom. This shortcoming in the paper is freely admitted. Finally, these concepts and such phrases as 'the management of innovation' and 'strategies of change' smack of manipulation, if not of a military exercise. One trusts that it will become clear that these terms, which now form part of conventional language of those who write about innovation, do not, in fact, imply any centralized agency manipulating individuals and institutions at the periphery.

### The patterns of curriculum change

The first model can be referred to as the *diffusion* pattern. Planned patterns of *curriculum* change have emerged only in recent years. In the past the major form of planned change was structural, where the government or LEA altered the institutional framework of education. The 'secret garden of the curriculum' was not the object of estate management. Innovation occurred by means of diffusion and was relatively unstructured. New ideas and practices spread through social networks of creators, 'product champions', opinion leaders and potential adopters. To some extent this was, and is, institutionalized through the roles played by HMI and LEA inspectors and through a whole variety of courses and conferences. But the key to the process was the response of the interested individual. It was no part of an overarching change strategy and differs from the more deliberate strategies of *dissemination* of new method and materials adopted more recently by various agencies of curriculum development. The diffusion pattern was characteristic of the British educational system and its *geist*. It was congruent with a decentralized structure, a faith in 'adhocracy' rather than bureaucracy, a confidence in the teacher (or, perhaps more correctly, the headteacher), and an emphasis on the importance of the autonomy of the school—within certain financial and policy constraints.

Little is known about the sources of *invention* in education, and not a great deal more is known about the process of *diffusion*, although current research by the Curriculum Diffusion Research Project of Chelsea College is adding to our knowledge. American research suggests that in the past the process of unplanned diffusion was slow. However, in recent years alternative patterns have emerged which have involved the central development of an innovation and its planned dissemination to the schools. This approach is now usually referred to as the Research, Development and Dissemination model (RD and D). A number of stages can be identified in theory, although in practice it is not always easy to separate them. Guba and Clark have suggested the following stages in the process:

Research—to provide the knowledge base for innovation
Development—to produce the innovation
Dissemination—to inform potential adopters about the innovations
Demonstration—to gain acceptance of the innovation by potential users through demonstrating its effectiveness
Implementation—to incorporate the innovation into the school
Institutionalization—to ensure that the innovation becomes a fully functioning part of the school—that it 'takes'

Havelock (1971) has suggested that the RD and D model has the following characteristics:

1  a *rational sequence* in the process
2  *planning*—on a massive scale over a considerable period of time
3  a *division and coordination* of labour—the use of various specialists in the process
4  an assumption that the consumer is both *rational* and *passive*
5  proponents who are willing to accept a high cost in the initial stages in anticipation of the benefits of *efficiency* and *quality*

Tony Becher (1971) of the Nuffield Foundation has pointed out that the model also assumes that the similarities between receiving schools are greater than their differences.

This strategy has been less successful than some protagonists hoped. Although there have been some relative successes (e.g. Nuffield Science materials were being used by over 45 per cent of schools with GCE forms within five years of their initial availability), two major problems have been encountered. One has been the distorting effect of *adaptation*. There is perhaps much to be said for the injunction to 'adopt and adapt', but adaptation has often meant 'knocking off the corners to get it through the doors of the school'. In other words, completely transforming the innovation in order to bring it into line with prevailing beliefs and procedures and thereby robbing it of its innovative character. Thus, materials intended for use as part of a discovery learning approach are used in traditionally didactic ways. The other problem has been the lack of sustained commitment to an innovation. Hence Ron Wastnedge's (1971) plaintive comment on Nuffield Junior Science that it is alive and well—in Ontario, Canada.

In the terminology of Guba and Clark (1965), the stage of institution-alization was not achieved here. There are several reasons why some projects do not achieve this stage. One is the inevitable shortage of resources. RD and D agencies have naturally put all their money into Research, Development and Dissemination. Another is the lack of congruence between, on the one hand, the rational, systematic and intellectualized RD and D approach and the idiosyncratic, intuitive and individualistic approach of many teachers. A third problem has been the too ready assumption that curriculum change would bring with it changes in teachers' values, professional relationships and attitudes to pupils—in short, a transformation in the 'pedagogical code' of the school. Finally, early RD and D approaches failed to 'take account of the system' as pointed out by Macdonald and Rudduck (1971).

A final point to be made before leaving the RD and D model is that it is relevant only to certain kinds of innovation, particularly those involving the production of materials or the development of hard-ware. It is not, of course, relevant to such innovations as mixed ability grouping or team teaching.

A third model is that which Havelock and others have termed the *problem-solving* approach. The perspective here is not from the central development agency but from the school itself. Some LEAS have adopted a policy of supporting local initiatives. It has been felt that schools are too remote from the centre of national development projects and that they should develop innovations at the grassroots level. Even in the case of regional projects some schools have felt isolated. Shipman (1969) who studied the Integrated Studies Pro-gramme based upon Keele University, reported that even within the fifty mile radius of the project, the schools on the periphery felt a lack of contact with the centre at Keele and with other schools.

Havelock has identified the following characteristics of the problem-solving model:

1 *need* (in this case the felt needs of the school) is taken as the starting point of innovation
2 need is translated into a specific *problem*
3 *diagnosis* is an important part of the process
4 the *internal resources* of the system are fully utilized before out-side resources are called upon
5 *self initiated* innovation has the best chance of survival

The problem-solving approach is being widely advocated at the present time. In his Reith lectures Donald Schon (1971) stressed the point that organizations should become 'learning systems', that is, they should develop the practice of looking both inwards in order to monitor the effectiveness of their own functioning and outwards in order to detect changes in their environment and become aware of innovations elsewhere which they might usefully adopt.

There is a compelling basic assumption to the problem-solving approach to innovation by schools, which is that teachers will become committed to the changes which they themselves have initiated. However, the strategy is not without its problems. One difficulty is that an innovation generated within a single school may not add to the body of professional good practice except through the rather chancy process of ad hoc diffusion. If educational situations *are* unique, then this is inevitable. But without accepting the view that particular innovation is appropriate to all schools at a given point in time, there are often so many factors common to different schools that an innovation developed by one may well be appropriate to many others. Education has not been particularly good at building a cumulative body of good practice. This is partly due to the problems of evaluation (and that is a separate question) but it is also partly due to the fact that our procedures for converting grassroots inventions into a common stock of educational knowledge are at the moment rudimentary. A second difficulty is that the problem-solving approach perhaps makes unwarranted assumptions about the level of expertise of the staff of a school. Clearly the fact has to be faced that not all teachers are capable of developing high quality curriculum materials, certainly not to the degree of the special development teams at local and regional levels. The problem-solving approach also makes the assumption that schools are able to generate from within the organizational patterns which characterize a 'learning system'. We thus have the propositions: innovation requires changes in the social system of the school; change in the social system of the school is a major innovation. This is the educational 'Catch 22'. In short, the problem-solving model has much to commend it, but if problem-solving is seen in terms of the individual school then it is unlikely to be successful unless the school can draw upon external materials, services and other forms of help from outside. The assumption is that the school will draw on such help, but the help must be there in a systematized form. However, before turning to an alternative strategy we can consider some of the problems of change at the school and teacher level which it must to some degree resolve.

*Problems of change at school and teacher levels*

Four problematic areas of change have been chosen for brief consideration: teachers' values, working relationships in school, the administrative structure of schools, and teacher professionalism.

The most fundamental form of innovation is the transformation of the values of teachers. All other forms of innovation—in materials, methods, pupil grouping and so forth—are often dependent for their success upon a shift in the values of teachers. The intimate relationship between teacher values and the effectiveness of a particular innovation is clearly brought out in Joan Barker Lunn's (1970) study of streaming in the primary school. At the present time we perhaps too readily make the assumption that to change the organization of a school, or its curriculum, or its architecture, will force teachers to reconsider their values and possibly change them. There is some justification for this assumption; a change of context can stimulate to a shift in values but this is not enough. There is an abundant sociopsychological literature on attitude change which points to the fact that it is likely to occur in an appropriate normative context, and this context consists of people. People's attitudes are changed by other people and this suggests the greater use of group methods in effecting value changes. It is far from axiomatic that teachers *will* undergo a value change in such circumstances, since group methods are not manipulative but are predicated on the assumption that values may *not* change.

Collaborative working relationships between teachers have in the past been rather restricted. The teacher has worked in the physically isolated setting of the classroom and his insulation from other teachers has been supported by the strong professional norm of non-interference. But the trend is towards a greater degree of integration of teachers at the level of their day to day work, brought about by the need to determine common objectives, team teaching, interdisciplinary enquiry, flexible grouping, open plan architecture and so forth. In the most successful innovatory situations whatever the basic strategy collaborative relationships can be achieved relatively painlessly: in an RD and D situation, development teams can establish good relationships with teachers and also create these between teachers, and successful problem-solving schools can generate collaborative relationships from within. But there are difficulties, and perhaps team teaching affords a good example where teachers have been attracted to an innovation without appreciating its full implications for professional relationships and the significance of the teacher's loss of autonomy.

A similar point can be made about change in the administration of schools. In the past the administration of British schools has been based upon a paradox. The head has enjoyed a high degree of authority in determining the goals of the school, but has had limited influence over the classroom activities of the teacher owing to the norm of noninterference. The teacher has enjoyed a high degree of classroom autonomy, but has had relatively little involvement in changing the goals of the school. This situation is changing, partly through the growing pressure for a greater involvement of teachers in the management of schools, which is part of a broader sociopolitical trend, and partly from the fact that the growing integration of teachers as the result of curriculum trends is stimulating a demand for collegial authority. Hence, many schools have created academic boards and a school like Countesthorpe has vested the running of the school in the staff 'moot'. The relationship between collegiality and innovativeness remains an open question, but a number of students of organizational change have noted the necessity of good 'organizational health' (Miles 1965) which involves clear goals, open communication, shared authority, cohesiveness, adaptability and high morale. This is relevant to the RD and D strategy since it is arguable that innovations will not 'take' in a school lacking these qualities. It is also relevant to the problem-solving strategy; the creation of such an organizational climate is a first priority since finding solutions to specific problems will be a function of it.

The final question concerns the professionalism of teachers. The available evidence suggests that, taken as a whole, teachers tend to have the following characteristics: they are atheoretical, unimpressed by research, influenced in their curriculum decisions by factors internal to the school, committed more to the 'joys of teaching' than to educational objectives, evaluate their own work subjectively, cherish their classroom autonomy and privacy, get their major satisfactions from their personal relationships with pupils, and approach teaching intuitively. But, as indicated in the earlier parts of this section, these attributes are under pressure. Perhaps one can very crudely distinguish two types of teacher professionalism: *restricted professionalism* (not using that term pejoratively) which refers to a high level of classroom competence, teaching skill and good relationships with pupils; and *extended professionalism* which embraces restricted professionalism but additionally embraces other attributes of a teacher. These include seeing his work in the wider context of community and society; ensuring that his work is informed by theory, research and current examplars of good practice; being willing to

*not professionalism at all*

collaborate with other teachers in teaching, curriculum development and the formulation of school policy; and having a commitment to keeping himself professionally informed. It is perhaps implicit in current trends in educational practice that there will be a concomitant shift from restricted to extended professionalism.

Each of the four problems considered in this section leads one to the view that, although individual schools can and should adopt a problem-solving orientation, they may need to have available to them in their search for solutions various agencies which they can call upon on a voluntary basis. Many schools will not successfully deal with the four problems discussed without help from elsewhere. This brings us to a consideration of an alternative strategy of innovation.

### A professional centre strategy

A number of terms can be, and have been, used to describe the institution which is the basis of the strategy to be considered here, e.g. regional resource centre, linkage centre. The term *professional centre* has been chosen because it is, of course, a concept introduced in the James Report. But it is also one which is capable of being extended beyond the model outlined there.

The basic premise is that there is a need for roles and institutions intermediate between the school and the agencies of curriculum change. Of course, such roles and institutions currently exist in considerable variety. There are the roles performed by LEA inspectors and advisers in this respect, but their functions vary considerably and we do not, in fact, know how much time inspectors and advisers have available to devote to supporting the innovative efforts of schools, nor how systematic this is. One would guess that this varies considerably both between authorities and between personnel within the same authority. There are also over 200 teachers centres, but again their actual functions with regard to supporting innovations in schools would appear to vary considerably. Some are agencies of diffusion of new ideas and practices amongst individual teachers. Others are involved in a much more systematic way with curriculum development in schools, and Allan Rudd describes perhaps the most ambitious of these schemes in his paper on the North West Curriculum Project.

A professional centre strategy would reinforce existing agencies. The base might be a teachers centre, college of education, university or polytechnic. Its functions *vis-à-vis* innovation might be *linkage, support, consultancy* and *in-service training*—although these four functions are only analytically distinctive and in practice they would be less distinguishable. We can consider the first three of these in this section and treat in-service separately in the final section.

The linkage function of the professional centre would be to act as an intermediate institution between national agencies of curriculum development and innovating schools. This function would thus form part of either an RD and D strategy or of a problem-solving strategy in that schools would have an obvious source of help. Some of the functions of the professional centre as linking agency would be to collect, exhibit and otherwise make available resources of various kinds (e.g. project materials, research findings) to act as a centre of information for what is happening in the locality, to act as a link between colleges, schools and other institutions where mutual benefit might be expected to ensue, and to create awareness of current innovation in schools through direct approaches, thus supplementing the current work of LEA inspectors and HMI.

A second function would be to provide continuous support for RD and D projects for participating schools after the withdrawal of the development team and for nonparticipating schools which would like help and guidance in the adoption and institutionalization of an innovation. This need was recognized some years ago (Smith 1966), but only limited progress has been made in meeting this need. Looking at the project support function of the professional centre from the problem-solving perspective, its functions might be seen as providing support—through arranging workshops, seminars, organizing the development and exchange of materials, and coordinating visits etc—for projects which develop beyond the single school.

A third function would be to provide a consultancy service. It would be the base for a permanent group of consultants (or, preferably, for successive groups of consultants since it is important that a consultancy service of this kind should be based upon seconded inspectors, heads and teachers to ensure the regular infusion of school experience) and act as an agency for people from the appropriate departments of colleges, polytechnics and universities (e.g. education, management, psychology, social administration and sociology departments) and from other institutions (e.g. research institutes, development agencies) who might be able to make a contribution towards assisting change.

It has been argued that schools—like industrial and commercial organizations, hospitals etc—often require help in the process of change. The currently fashionable terms for such helpers is *change agent* (Hoyle 1971) but this term perhaps connotes a directive role which would, in fact, be quite inappropriate. The change agent role is essentially nondirective and thus not at odds with the problem-solving orientation of the school. Summarizing an anlysis presented elsewhere (Hoyle 1970), it can be said that the two main targets of change are the curriculum and the social system of the school. The latter would include *perspectives* (attitudes, knowledge, beliefs, skills etc) *relationships* (between head, teachers, pupils) and *organization* (goals, structure, administration). The services which the consultant might provide are theory, analysis, research and the provision of support (e.g. workshops, courses, expertise). The consultant would work together with the school staff—or part of it—as a group, both in the centre and, importantly, in the school itself as it goes about its task. The consultant would need to have two kinds of knowledge—curriculum knowledge and behavioural science knowledge. This perhaps argues for a consultancy *team*, rather than an individual.

There are, undoubtedly, great problems here, given the autonomy of the British school and the often legitimate suspicions which many heads and teachers have of outside 'experts'. One big difficulty is, therefore, one of access. But, as the relationship would be voluntary and collaborative, this might be overcome in time. The other is the shortage of expertise, of people who have curriculum knowledge and who also know something of the social psychology of organizations. The number of people who have these two kinds of expertise is growing, and the problems might be partly solved when a professional centre can draw upon the resources of a college, university or polytechnic.

One is not underestimating the difficulties which a professional centre would face in providing linkage, support and consultancy functions—especially the latter—but they are, perhaps, problems which should be faced.

### In-service training and the professional centre strategy

The fourth function of the professional centre strategy, the provision of in-service training, is the concern of the final section of the paper. Three propositions regarding in-service training will be advanced.

The first is that in-service training should to some degree be carried out by the school itself. Clearly the school cannot meet all the training requirements of teachers. Teachers need to develop their knowledge, skills and perspectives in a wider context than can be provided by a single school; innovation is dependent upon this. At the same time, a school should organize its own staff development programme.

A second proposition is that the in-service training of teachers at the school level can be usefully linked to a specific innovation. Ron Pepper (1972) has given an account of the in-service programme at Thomas Calton School. This included, amongst other staff activities, a concern with the team-based integrated studies—a curriculum innovation in the school.

A third proposition is that the focus of school-linked in-service training should be the functioning group: an entire school staff, subject department, an interdisciplinary teaching team or an academic board. Most in-service provision at the moment is aimed at individuals who may share common interests but who are only infrequently working partners in the same school. This is entirely appropriate in the case of much in-service work. On the other hand, where the in-service training is concerned with innovations which need to be operated at school, department or team level, there is always the problem of the enthusiastic individual returning from the course and trying to 'sell' the innovation to his less committed colleagues who have not attended. Many industrial training schemes are aimed at operating groups.

The professional centre strategy would appear to have much to offer to this sort of in-service work. For instance, if a school were contemplating a major innovation—such as introducing mixed ability grouping of integrated studies—the professional centre could help to train staff in a number of ways. First of all, the centre could provide the setting for the meetings of school staff away from school. Matthew Miles has referred to the importance of 'temporary systems' where people meet away from the pressures of their normal working environment in order to discuss innovation in a more relaxed setting. Secondly, the professional centre staff could provide a support programme of reading, seminars, workshops, visits, assessments of research, and group work. Thirdly, the centre staff concerned with this training programme could act as change agents in the school itself. Such an approach would be more fruitful than some of the current hit-or-miss in-service programmes that we have at present. It should not be seen as a group of centre 'experts' imposing their ideas. To a large extent the school would be responsible for its own self-analysis and staff training, but the centre staff would be available to provide the resources which might not be available to the school.

## Conclusion

The argument of this paper has been that the problems of innovation perhaps cannot be resolved by either the RD and D or problem-solving strategies alone. Roles and institutions outside the school can, on the basis of voluntary collaboration, provide a resource which schools might call upon to assist their innovative activity. It has been proposed that a professional centre could coordinate much of the activity and, further, could be the base for in-service training which should increasingly be linked to school programmes of innovation and involve functioning groups of teachers rather than individuals.

On the other hand, it will be recognized that the paper has dodged some of the fundamental problems raised by this approach: its possibly overrationalistic basis, the whole question of resources, the problem of careers, especially for professional centre staff, and the source of incentives for innovation.

## References

BECHER, A. (1971) The dissemination and implementation of educational innovation. Paper read at the meeting of the British Association, Swansea, 1971

GUBA, E. and CLARK, D. L. (1965) An examination of potential change roles in education quoted in *Strategies in Educational Change Newsletter no. 2* Ohio State University, October

HAVELOCK, R. G. (1971) The utilization of educational research and development *British Journal of Educational Technology* 2, 2

HOYLE, E. (1970) Planned organizational change in education *Research in Education* 3, May

HOYLE, E. (1971) 'The role of the change agent in educational innovation' in J. Walton (ed) *Curriculum Organization and Design* London: Ward Lock Educational

LUNN, J. BARKER (1970) *Streaming in the Primary School* Slough: NFER

MACDONALD, B. and RUDDUCK, J. (1971) Curriculum research and development projects: barriers to success *British Journal of Educational Psychology* 41, 2

MILES, M. B. (1965) 'Planned change and organizational health: figure and ground' in R. O. Carlson (ed) *Change Processes in the Public Schools* Eugene: University of Oregon Centre for the Advanced Study of Educational Administration

PEPPER, R. (1971) In-service training and the Thomas Calton School, Peckham *Forum* 14, 2

SCHON, D. A. (1971) *Beyond the Stable State: Public and Private Learning in a Changing Society* London: Temple Smith

SHIPMAN, M. (1969) Order and innovation in schools *New Society* 18th December

SMITH, R. IRVINE (1966) Curriculum reform *New Society* 12th May

WASTNEDGE, R. (1971) What happened to Nuffield Junior Science? *Where* 59, July

# 10 The diffusion of Schools Council curriculum development projects

## Tony Light

The Schools Council was established in 1964, taking over the work of the Secondary School Examinations Council and the Curriculum Study Group. In other words, we are barely eight years old—an important fact.

The Lockwood Report (Ministry of Education 1964) set out the terms of reference for the Council, and these were adopted without alteration. The opening paragraphs state:

> The objects of the Schools Council for the Curriculum and Examinations are to uphold and interpret the principle that each school should have the fullest possible measure of responsibility for its own work, with its own curriculum and teaching methods based on the needs of its own pupils and evolved by its own staff....
>
> In order to promote these objects, the Council will keep under review curricula, teaching methods and examinations in primary and secondary schools....

The individual responsibility of the school is thus placed first, and the task of reviewing curricula and examinations is firmly subordinated to the primary objective.

The activities of the Council are therefore directed towards enabling teachers to exercise greater choice within the curriculum. The Council stands for devolution and the acceptance of local responsibility so that while it promotes curriculum development at the national level, the Council recognizes that LEAs, schools and teachers will need to make provision at the local level in response to local situations—and that in the long term, curricular decisions will only be sustained by local resources.

The Schools Council has no authority over teachers. It attempts to exercise *influence* and to *encourage* developments within the curriculum, so that although sometimes it appears somewhat frustrating not to be able to prescribe a particular course of action, nevertheless the Council's recommendations and publications must stand on their intrinsic merit and not by any status which the Council confers. This is entirely proper, for it leaves the teacher freer to make his own choice from a widening range of materials, to exercise his own judgment and to create his own curriculum from a variety of sources.

## Functions of the Council

The functions of the Council are fourfold—research, development, dissemination and coordination—and these functions are exercised in the two major fields of interest: on the one hand curriculum, and on the other examinations. It is dangerous to try to draw a boundary between these two, for in fact the Council's policy is to see both curriculum and examinations as part of a whole process and to let neither dominate the scene.

The *research* function embraces enquiry into aspects of learning, research connected with curriculum development itself—the evaluation of teacher and pupil material—and also includes the scrutiny of development proposals; research in the examination field is also sponsored by the Council. The research is carried out both centrally and through projects.

The Council is best known however for its *development* projects and these form the major part of the Council's activities. A project develops a life of its own, and this will be discussed later. Additionally the Council is responsible for *disseminating* ideas and information about projects. Recently this aspect of the Council's work has become of major importance as indicated by the establishment of a large information section and by the establishment of a working party concerned with dissemination.

The fourth function is that of coordination. This particularly applies to the examinations field where the developmental work of the GCE and CSE Boards is to some extent coordinated by the Council's committees and officers.

It is consistent with our pluralistic approach that projects show a wide variety in their approach and scale. Two preconditions seem to be necessary: first that a clear need for curriculum development in a particular field should exist. This may be identified by research or enquiries, or by expressions of such need on the part of, for example, teachers' groups. The second precondition is that a project should be supported and confirmed in its work by the active interest, involvement and sympathetic criticism of a large number of teachers. In other words it should grow out of a grassroots concern and be seen to be relevant to the teacher's work in the classroom.

In the early years of national curriculum development these needs were most apparent in mathematics and science; and (following on the work of the Nuffield Foundation) the Schools Council involved itself in these subject areas as well as in the field of modern languages. The pressing needs of ROSLA engaged the Council from its birth, and many projects were established in order to provide new curricula for the emerging fifth and sixth forms. There is now an emphasis on examinations, and a continuing concern for meeting the particular needs of specific groups such as slow learners, or pupils in multiracial schools.

Because of this variety of approach it is difficult to draw up any typology of curriculum strategy. Each project tends to choose its own strategy and not to conform to a particular model. Its strategy will depend upon the task in hand and its resources. Most of the early projects relied fairly heavily on the research, development and dissemination model. More recently projects have shown variations on this standard theme and are moving towards greater involvement of teachers (the social interaction model) or client-centred strategies. However there are elements common to nearly all development projects.

The first is that of the trial school. Projects which hope to produce materials for teachers or pupils invariably establish a network of trial schools. The Council staff helps in this recruitment, advising projects on the distribution of schools to produce a representative sample. Additionally associate schools become involved with the project, and these together with the trial schools act as important agents of diffusion. The involvement of the trial schools and teachers working in them is perhaps the most crucial element in the whole of a project's life and the feedback from the trial schools leads to considerable modification of the project's material.

Linked with trials, the second common aspect of project life is the involvement of teachers in the work of the project. Projects are initiated as a response to needs and demands expressed by teachers and researchers. However projects often have a life of three or four years before any material emerges. This time lag may have serious repercussions, for unless the project has involved teachers on the way there may be an element of irrelevance about a project's findings and its publications. If for example a project starting in 1968 produces no materials for general use by teachers until 1972, other problems have arisen in the schools and the needs may have been overtaken by a succession of other events. This conclusion suggests that involvement of teachers during a project life is vital in terms of maintaining the dynamic of curriculum development. So one of the criteria for the success of a project would seem to be the degree to which it has been able to involve teachers in the production of materials.

The third common element is that of training. Most projects organize courses arranged to induct teachers into the procedures connected with their own project. These training courses or workshops become an important element in the diffusion process.

It is worth noting here that development and training are inextricably bound together. At its lowest level training involves the acquisition and mastery of techniques for use within the classroom. At a higher level, many projects are concerned with the approach of teachers and their attitudes towards new curricula, and some projects will be primarily concerned to encourage changes of attitude by teachers who attend their training courses. This interlocking nature of development and training poses somewhat of a dilemma for the Council. Training per se is peripheral to the *function* of the Council, for it recognizes that there are agencies or providers of training, notably the ATO and colleges and LEAs. Nevertheless the adoption of new techniques and changes of attitude induced by training is central to the *concern* of the Council.

Now both these points, i.e. the inextricability of development and training on the one hand and the desirability of involvement on the other, raise issues which are important within the context of the future in-service training programme and the professional development of the teacher. It strikes me that more flexibility is required within the system to enable teachers to grow professionally not merely through attendance at in-service courses but by involvement in curriculum development. We should be looking for many more ways of satisfying teachers than merely through work in the classroom or attendance on courses. The service of teachers should be recognized as varied and rich, including curriculum preparation, planning and development, as well as work in the classroom.

We now turn to diffusion and the Schools Council's central contribution to this process. I have already mentioned that projects develop a life of their own in which diffusion of ideas is one important aspect. However projects die, project teams disperse and teachers still require both information and access to the ideas which they have generated. Now the death of a project is not a tragic event if during its life there has been adequate attention paid to diffusion aspects. Increasingly we are asking projects to build this in to their total programme so that at the end of the day teachers have the necessary information and resources on which to make their choices.

This kind of situation is becoming more significant, and therefore the Council is having to take on some central responsibility for the aftercare of projects and to ensure through its own dissemination processes that teachers obtain information and advice. It is to consider all these particular aspects that the working party on dissemination was set up this year. Its considerations are likely to follow three particular directions. These are first the dissemination of information and ideas by the Council, second the establishment of networks for dissemination and the exchange of information, and third the adoption by schools of curriculum project material and ideas.

### Dissemination

As the work of the Council became more widely known and its projects began to disseminate their ideas, so the demand for information about the Council and its activities has grown. It was in response to these demands that the Information Section was established in 1970. This section comprises a central library of project materials and a permanent exhibition of teaching materials produced both by the projects and the Council. Supporting this central resource is distribution of information pamphlets, a regular news magazine *Dialogue*, and the answering of enquiries which flow into the Council by telephone and through visits to Great Portland Street. The range and variety of these enquiries has grown considerably since the establishment of the Information Section, and it is becoming increasingly obvious that not all enquiries or requirements can be met by the kind of general information provided on a broadsheet. There is therefore a need to be more discriminating in the kind of information we give in order to satisfy particular customers. This raises a fundamental question about this particular area of our work. Are we product-based or customer-based? It is obviously incumbent upon the Council to promote and encourage the use of its teaching materials. Nevertheless some would say that this approach is not as important as that of securing the greater interest and involvement of teachers in the whole life of the Council. Whichever approach should receive greater emphasis, there is certainly the need to know more about the process whereby the customer is encouraged to adopt the project materials and if we are to be client-orientated we certainly need to know more about the clients' needs and to be increasingly sensitive to them.

It is partly in meeting this need to be increasingly sensitive to teachers' requirements and also in tapping the grassroots that the teachers centres have proved so valuable. These have been established by the local authorities and are supported entirely by local budgets and often organized by teachers themselves, so that although the Schools Council has advocated their establishment, teachers centres are very much a local institution and exemplify the kind of devolution for which the Council stands. Teachers centres have also become the location for the dissemination of information about projects, for in-service courses and for curriculum development. Here again development work springs not merely from Council projects but from teachers' groups, as a result of wardens' or advisers' initiative, or as a result of courses operated by ATOs within the centres.

Naturally there is a range of standards both in provision and in work undertaken. This range is dependent to a large extent upon the absence or presence of a full-time warden. The least work seems to be achieved where the warden is on a part-time basis and where the centre is confined in its resources. The greatest influence seems to be where the centres are large and offer a variety of resources for the teacher, and where wardens are working alongside LEA advisers. Teachers centres therefore form a meeting point for Schools Council officers, for project directors and their teams, and the teachers themselves.

Teachers often say they find the Schools Council a rather vague kind of institution, hardly known and rarely understood. It was in order to make the Council better known and understood that field officers were appointed to visit schools within their regions to acquaint teachers with the work of the Council and to bring back to the Council requests and ideas. At present there are eleven field officers covering the whole country. With such a small number it is impossible for field officers to meet all teachers or indeed visit more than a handful of schools within their own region.

*Networks*
The implication is that since the Schools Council officers and project directors are limited in this respect, other ways must be found of ensuring that teachers are kept in touch and that requested information about curriculum development is available through alternative networks. It is therefore a major task of the working party on dis-

semination to identify those networks which will be most helpful in meeting teachers' needs.

We have therefore been exploring with all the providers, the possibilities of meeting these long-term needs by the establishment of a network of support. We have been anxious to identify the key people who might operate within this network and are presently looking for advice and help from local authority inspectors and advisers from the colleges of education and from ATO in-service tutors. All these groups have had opportunities of visiting the Council and we are presently meeting with ATCDE, UCET, NAIEO representatives to look at this whole question of networks for diffusion.

The form that this network might take is as yet unclear, and will depend greatly on the outcomes from the James Report and the reorganization of local authorities. Coupled with the need for a network is the need to establish alternative and supplementary resources to those of the teachers centres; to identify in James's terms those centres for professional activity which will enable development to be enhanced by the concentration of resources. In this field of planning, as in all those activities mentioned so far, the Schools Council would hope to make a contribution.

*Schools*
The third area of concern, that of the school, is to some extent the most intriguing. Curriculum development obviously takes place in schools. The school is the adopting system, and it is within the school, within each classroom, that the fruits of development will be seen, and not only of curriculum development but also of in-service training. We are all aware I expect of the limitations of in-service courses which withdraw teachers from the classroom and seek to give them techniques and ideas hoping that when they return to school these ideas and techniques will be put into practice. We have no guarantee that this in fact will be so, for each teacher will be subject to factors and constraints which operate within the school. The head may be unsympathetic to new ideas; there may be limited resources; the timetable may not permit experiment; a whole array of internal and external constraints affect the teacher and his work in the classroom. I mention here the working party on the whole curriculum which, within its brief of reviewing the whole curriculum of the thirteen to sixteen age range, is also looking at these factors and constraints, and seeking to clarify such important procedures within the school as decision-making, curriculum planning, timetable compilation. In some way it is fortuitous that these two working parties (i.e. whole

curriculum and dissemination) are both operating at the same time. This is a most happy coincidence, for both are of vital and interdependent importance. They create as it were the towers of the bridge between the Council with its central function and the school with its local responsibility for curriculum development. The structure linking these towers is the network of support and activity which has been briefly mentioned above. The metaphor is crude and in one major respect inadequate—its imagery is too static and mechanistic. Curriculum development as we well know is both dynamic and organic.

Like other English institutions, much of our activity has been empirical and pragmatic in character; we have looked for practical solutions to problems as they have arisen and tried to identify as we have gone along those areas in which we need to deploy our resources.

This pragmatic approach, whilst eminently successful in some ways, has its limitations and what we now need, I suggest, is a programme of research which will identify problems, concerns and possible directions for both development and diffusion. We need for example not only to evaluate projects' outcomes and materials as we have been doing with recent projects, but also to evaluate the process itself and discover how effective projects are in the *diffusion* of their ideas. We need more research about diffusion strategies in the field of education. Most of the present experience seems to be derived from agricultural or health programmes. Whilst it is interesting to know how contraception methods have been diffused in Puerto Rico, or how the farmers of the midwest of the United States have adopted hybrid wheat strains, nevertheless we need much more work which is directly related to what goes on in schools and with teachers. We need to look more carefully at the ways in which schools operate, how each part of their system reacts with the other, and what kinds of effect innovations have upon schools. We need to know more about the innovating schools and about the role of consultancy in helping schools to arrive at solutions to problems which they have identified. All these aspects are likely to be of considerable interest in the future.

I shall summarize by making three points about the role of the Council. First, the Council's activities need to be seen *in relation to clients* if we are to give true expression to the concept of devolution and the desirability of teachers making more curricular decisions. We need to be able to support the teacher much more with information, with access to ideas, resources and a range of supporting agencies which will help him in his work.

Second, because we are principally concerned with helping teachers adapt to and adopt new ways we are therefore much concerned for the professional development of the teacher. This means making a contribution towards the thinking about in-service training, and possibly, because of our central function and national perspective, aiding the growth of regional networks whereby professional development is fostered.

Finally as we stand for devolution and for the professional development of the teacher, so we also to some extent epitomize, or should epitomize, the aspirations of the teacher towards what can be called the progressive or innovatory end of the education continuum. By sustaining an enquiring stance between the established traditional and the innovatory progressive poles of this continuum we hope to encourage research, experiment, and debate which will foster the stating of aims and objectives leading to a richer, relevant and satisfying education for our pupils. The achievement of these goals requires a partnership of the kind which we have tried to build over the last eight years, and which we will continue to build in the future.

*References*

MINISTRY OF EDUCATION (1964) *Schools' Curricula and Examinations* (Lockwood Report) London: HMSO

# 11 Local curriculum development

## Allan Rudd

*An exercise in partnership*
The James Report envisages local curriculum development and
evaluation as one important type of third cycle activity, through
which teachers can extend their personal education, develop their
professional competence and improve their understanding of educational principles and techniques. Such work (among other types)
would go on in a network of professional centres, each under the
leadership of a full-time professional warden who enjoyed an
independent role. The work of these centres would involve bringing
into partnership diverse agencies—schools, universities, polytechnics,
colleges of education, advisory services, teachers centres, resource
centres and further education institutions—notably in helping to
staff the professional centre. The basic principles of this proposal
bear a marked resemblance to those on which local teachers centres
were established in north-west England during 1967, though the
scale of activities now proposed is greatly in excess of that realized
to date in teachers centres:

> There are two basic principles in which progress on curriculum
> development should be built: first, that motive power should
> come primarily from local groups of teachers accessible to one
> another; second, that there should be effective and close colla-
> boration between teachers and all those who are able to offer
> cooperation. There is no hierarchy of initiative or control. The
> cooperative effort of each interest needs to be involved in equal
> partnership, and all parties should be ready to give or to seek
> support. (Schools Council 1967)

This paper presents a critique of some aspects of the North West
Regional Curriculum Development Project, in terms of certain of
the James principles. But before doing so I must affirm my own basic

H

belief about teacher education, which shortage of space prevents me from attempting to justify. I believe that teachers learn in fundamentally the same manner as do their pupils. If we really expect them to adopt demonstrably better procedures in the classroom we must set up appropriate conditions for establishing and maintaining the new behaviours. Just as telling pupils how to carry through a task is not a sufficient condition for ensuring pupil mastery of that task, so merely telling teachers how to improve their teaching or presenting them with persuasive propaganda about the merits of particular techniques is unlikely by itself to lead to improved teaching. I regard it as axiomatic that the teacher who learns from his own (appropriate) experience understands in a way which is just not available to persons who merely try to follow the instructions of others or who seek to please their superiors. For experience-based innovation not only promotes increased pedagogical skill; from the manner in which the new skill is accumulated the teacher also learns concurrently the art of mastering new professional skills, and that confidence and sureness of touch which are hallmarks of the full professional. In short, I see the local curriculum development group as a setting within which teachers can become the willing agents of their own continuing professional education.

*Task orientation*
The North West Project is a consortium of fifteen teachers centres established and maintained by thirteen LEAs, most centres being supported jointly by two LEAs. The whole enterprise is coordinated through the University of Manchester Area Training Organization; but except for major committees, all the project's work is carried on in one or other of the teachers centres. When the project was launched early in 1967 few educationists in the region (or elsewhere in the country) had many clearly developed ideas as to how such centres might run, and a good question was (and remains) 'Why should teachers take their professional concerns to local teachers centres?'

The academic answer usually given is that such centres provide like-minded teachers with a local and relatively unstructured setting within which to discuss professional matters, often as a preliminary to proposing innovations within their own school setting. Yet five years later it has to be confessed that most such centres are still bedevilled by the problem of how to entice teachers into the centres for sustained bouts of professional work. Short in-service courses, exhibitions of teaching materials or of pupils' work, a reference library/resource centre, a workshop for making needed apparatus—

all are valuable services for a teachers centre to offer. It has been our experience, however, that creative work in curriculum development provides much the strongest stimulus for schools' commitment to the work of teachers centres. In turn such commitment provides the teachers centre with the life-space it needs if it is to function positively in its local area.

From our experience the teachers centre leader who wishes to stimulate creative work in curriculum planning would do well to concentrate attention on the critical areas of teacher concern, viz pupil needs and interests and the demands which society makes on its young people. This is where commitment can begin; and it is only by dealing with the significant concerns of teachers that a professional centre can win recognition as a worthwhile focus for local professional effort.

The leader who succeeds in winning such life-space may well find that the issue which a group of teachers brings to his centre seems so vast, so complex and so basic that the working group despairs of its own capacity to contribute anything substantial to the problem's solution. In reply, the leader may argue that by pooling their knowledge, by drawing upon particular individual skills and by extending their thought as they interact with other educationists, the group will achieve much more than could have been obtained by any one member working in isolation. Though teachers may be impressed they will not necessarily be convinced by such arguments; for they are, rightly, jealous of those demands upon professional time which interfere with their primary task, that of planning and guiding their pupils' learning. This implies that any professional centre's first development scheme must be, and be seen to be, successful. The scheme need not be large, but it must deal with a real and urgent issue facing a definable group of teachers in the area, must appear from the outset to be well organized, must achieve its intermediate targets and must yield a product which demonstrates unequivocally the advantages of teachers cooperating for professional purposes.

The North West Project has derived much continued goodwill from teachers and LEAs in the region over a period of several years by focussing its effort on the ROSLA problem, by maintaining several groups working in parallel (so that the anticipated total product would exceed the sum of its parts) and by meeting intermediate targets published before the project began.

There is of course no lack of suitable focal points for professional effort. Local schemes for combining two secondary into one comprehensive school, for preparing pupils for examination under a new syllabus or for introducing counsellors into an Authority's schools are but three examples of situations where innovations initiated outside the school put strong pressure on identifiable groups of teachers to modify traditional practices. Less demanding of change, but no less stimulating towards innovation, are the curriculum products published for the Schools Council or the findings of research carried out by NFER or similar bodies. An alert professional centre leader will seek to grasp such 'teachable moments' and to fan a spark of passing interest into a steadily burning flame of commitment to inquiry, one capable of sustaining and directing effort over a period of time.

*Provision of needed resources*
Once the development task has been given and accepted, adequate resources need to be provided for the work. These fall under three main headings: manpower, finance and support services. Only passing reference will be made here to questions of manpower, important as these are. It is a basic principle of local development work that teacher participation be voluntary. Two implications of this principle are: that the dynamics and the climate of a working group must be constructive and satisfying (rather than merely congenial); and that in an extended enterprise, such as the North West Project, regular opportunities have to be provided for group membership to change. Though in theory the latter implication might bring about dissipation of accumulating experience, this circumstance has never arisen in the North West Project.

At no time has the project distinguished among types of teachers when panel members were being recruited. We have sought heterogeneous groups, whose members come from varying professional backgrounds. The enthusiasm and energy of the young have been as valued as the experience and wisdom of more senior teachers; and we have found that groups of such heterogeneity have ensured that a wide range of interests, ideas and suggestions is taken into account in reaching decisions. Now, near the end of the fifth year of development work, about one quarter of current panel membership consists of founder members, with another quarter having joined the project when field trials began, and since remained with us.

Though it is a cardinal principle of the North West Project that all curriculum development work be controlled by teachers, such control could be absolute only were the teachers themselves to underwrite project finances. In the early days the work was substantially, though not entirely, supported by finance from the Schools Council; but collectively the thirteen LEAS concerned have provided more than

£200,000 of public money to support the project's work. Thus ways have had to be found to make possible the essential freedoms development panels need, within the normal rules and practices of LEA financial administration.

For accounting purposes each project team (of which there were seven) has been regarded as an educational unit (such as a school), with the panel chairman being cast in the role of headmaster. Estimates of proposed expenditure for the financial year 1969–70 (for example) and forecasts for the year 1970–71, based upon discussions between panel chairman, panel members and project director, were compiled according to the codes of expenditure in normal LEA use. Those familiar with LEA procedures will know that the financial year 1969–70 began in April 1969 and that, if the needed finance were to be available then, estimates would have to be submitted in October 1968—just one month after the development panel had first met to plan and carry through its 1968–69 year's work. Thus each panel's first major activity involved making detailed predictions as to the form, content and extent of the field studies it was to undertake during the 1969–70 school year, since money for providing teaching kits to be used in these studies had to come from funds then being estimated. Since the writing of a course worthy of field trials and the accumulation of a suitable teaching kit for this course were to be the focus of the year's panel work which was only then beginning, it is not difficult to appreciate the frustration among developers to which this demand might have given rise, however necessary this procedure was in the eyes of administrators.

The source of such possible irritation was removed, however, when the project's finance and general purposes committee agreed to group estimates into a small number of codes, and later to allow virement between codes and between years on each panel's account. These latter two provisions are believed to be outside the strict code of LEA rules, though within the discretionary powers available to administrators. The element of freedom introduced by these changes made it possible for panels at all times to approach their development task without any serious financial constraint on their planning.

This example illustrates beautifully the creative role which a liberal administration can play in local curriculum development work. However, if one is to generalize on the basis of this single example, two additional points need to be stressed. First, that administrative initiatives such as this are likely only when a basis of mutual trust and a sense of common purpose exist between developers and administrators. Second, that an important element in such trust is administrative competence on the part of the project executive (i.e. the professional centre leader); in particular, his ability to persuade panel chairmen to budget prudently and wisely in the first instance, rather than to follow the common practice of submitting estimates greatly in excess of what the panel is likely to need, against the chance of across the board reductions before these estimates are approved.

Teacher control of local development work is a principle to which much thought has been given in the North West Project. Coupled with the need for adequate representation of all other interests involved in a wide-ranging and complex regional experiment, the principle inevitably implies a steering committee, which is more effective as a reaction group than as a discussion group. Yet over the period under review the committee, far from degenerating into a mere 'talking shop' has proved a striking example of the processes of democratic control of a many-sided exercise. The fact is that at most meetings there have been serious matters for consideration, and discussion has never been cut short by the chairman. Papers on a great variety of topics have been presented for consideration, and have received the benefit of close scrutiny by a large number of people from different backgrounds.

Committee papers are prepared in the regional study group, an executive body comprising the project director, the deputy director, and leaders of all fifteen teachers centres. Anticipation of close scrutiny in committee, and knowing that the eventual decision will have to be given effect by the executive, ensures careful planning in all matters. This organization also has the merit of keeping open *three* channels of communication between teachers and steering committee: via teachers' associations; via LEA administrations; and via teacher centre leaders (who are nonvoting members of steering committee).

Without doubt the most notable feature of the steering committee has been the relationship with its finance and general purposes committee. A school normally functions within a financial framework established by its LEA, one which generally bears little close relationship to the curricula proposed by the teaching staff of that school. In the North West Project, however, the finance and general purposes committee has functioned within a framework of general policy and curriculum proposals decided by a steering committee on which LEAS (even collectively) had only minority representation. The novelty of this relationship, and its success as a working organization, provide striking evidence of the spirit of initiative and cooperation, shown by both elected and professional LEA representatives throughout the life of the project.

*Support for working groups*
An important asset of group work in local curriculum development centres is that each teacher brings to the group his own background of knowledge, skill and ability to think. These qualities offer great scope for studying curriculum problems because, when given the opportunity to think about his work, a teacher has greater potential than an outsider for promoting change, because he knows his own situation, its dynamics and the need for improvement. The problem under review has personal meaning for him. However, this asset may turn into something of a liability, should an emerging identity induce the group to adopt a narrow interpretation of its problem, and to become impervious to suggestions originating outside the group.

One way of avoiding this situation developing is to include among the group teachers crossing traditional lines of association and pockets of thinking. For example, it would have been very stimulating to have had a few primary school teachers among the North West Project's panel membership; but the pattern of release for panel work made this difficult to achieve. Another method, of which some but not enough use was made, is to include in each panel's programme events designed to extend professional insights, e.g. reviews of relevant literature, visits to schools where interesting work is taking place.

A third method, in which the project became very effective, was based on functions in which panel representatives met other teachers from schools in the region. Almost always such meetings were held for specific purposes, e.g. to recruit teachers for panel work or schools for field trials; but this purpose was always set in the general context of reporting back to teachers an outline of current plans, policies and proposed courses of action. Wherever possible these meetings were kept small, were held in teachers centres and were led by members of the development panel concerned. Despite their informality, the challenge of presenting the panel's ideas to an informed and critical audience always put panel members on their mettle. Not every member welcomed the prospect of such meetings, but all prepared thoroughly for them. Afterwards many members reported deriving new insights from the encounter, and in the end felt a thrill in realizing their ability to hold and convince such an audience as to the value of the general thrust of their panel's work.

The regional study group has played a crucial role in supporting local development work. In the early days the discrepancy in leadership experience between the project director and the newly-appointed leaders of local centres was vast. The latter had for the most part been recruited straight from the classroom, often on a temporary basis; and they were given the task of establishing and maintaining centres for which few models then existed. At that time, therefore, the regional study group became excessively director-centred, the local centre leaders being both professionally and emotionally overdependent. Within a year, however, the professional confidence of local leaders began visibly to grow, as they realized their ability to describe (and where necessary to defend) the project's ideas to teachers in their areas, and as the centres themselves became increasingly acceptable as focal points for local, as well as regional, initiative. This proved a very difficult time in the regional study group, as each local leader struggled to achieve more autonomy during discussions of both educational and administrative matters. Such struggles generally arose when individuals or subgroups invested great personal and professional capital in ideas which seemed to others unlikely to chime with the wider educational purposes of the project.

At such times it would have been very easy for the project director to have adopted either an excessively dominant or recessive style of leadership. Respectable arguments were not lacking to support either approach, for example:

1 The project had been set up to carry out a specific programme of work within a given period of time, and it was important to work within these terms of reference.
2 The project had been established to study the feasibility of groups of teachers working as curriculum developers. Such groups had first to 'learn the trade'; and the short-term role of leadership was to teach the needed skills. If the project were to fail to demonstrate the competence of teacher groups for such work, the inhibiting effect of that failure upon curriculum development work within the region (and perhaps also elsewhere) might be very great indeed.
3 Where appointed leaders were unable to convince their groups of the wisdom of proposed courses of action, each group should be allowed to go its own way, and to learn from its own (perhaps bitter) experience.

In the director's view, the project had to concern itself with all three of these major purposes (products, feasibility and training); and the result was that at this time regional study group meetings sometimes became very exhausting encounters indeed. It is therefore appropriate at this point to recognize the high degree of commitment and energy (both intellectual and emotional) which the local leaders brought to this work, from which they learned above all else how to create and maintain a humane yet purposeful climate for local development work.

Perhaps the most lasting problem with which the North West Project has struggled is that of making available to development panels the knowledge, wisdom and skill which specialist educationists are anxious to place at panels' disposal. At an early stage in its life the project drew up and circulated extensive lists of such persons and institutions, leaving to panels themselves the initiative for seeking such support. It must be reported that these services have only very rarely been called for.

For much of its life morale in the panels, as well as among centre leaders, has been dominated by a feeling which might be expressed thus: 'For the first time groups of teachers have been given the opportunity to show what they can do as curriculum developers—and by God, we're going to show them!' Even the project director, when visiting a panel, has occasionally been asked, half-jocularly 'Have you come to tell us what to do?' The tone of voice in which the question is asked may indicate either resentment at the apparent suggestion that in any crisis leadership passes out of teachers' hands, or relief that in an emergency an authority figure is willing to come to the rescue. The question itself epitomizes the difficulties inherent in introducing outside consultants into local development panels.

This determination of teachers to throw off the (perceived) weight of imposed authority is one of the most persuasive features of the climate within which the project has operated. The source of perceived authority may vary, embracing, for example, traditional school practices, the pressure of new curriculum orthodoxies, the weight of the standard literature, the thrust of advice given by those in positions of authority in the educational system. The response to the pressure from outside has always been the same: 'Why should we? We want to do it our way. Let us experiment for ourselves.' The parallels between this response and that of any young person discovering some new insight or developing some new skill are striking, and provide (at least for the project director), convincing evidence of the value of local curriculum development work as in-service education. Once more it is necessary to affirm a belief (for which the project now has a good deal of supporting evidence) that teachers who learn by discovery and learn to discover are more likely to establish subsequently in their classrooms conditions in which their pupils can do likewise.

Nevertheless, a curriculum development project is concerned with products as well as with processes; and it would be a sign of increasing professional maturity when a panel felt sufficiently confident in itself to state in effect: 'As a panel we do not know enough about the problem with which we are trying to cope. Please come and give us your advice as to how we might best proceed.' It is encouraging to be able to report that in general panels in the North West Project have for the past year or so felt sufficiently mature to seek such support informally through their acquaintances, if not yet formally from available professional sources.

## A humane working climate

Any professional centre leader finding himself in this position will give a great deal of his attention to creating in his centre circumstances likely to foster such emerging professional maturity. Experience in the North West Project suggests the importance for such outcomes of a humane working climate.

A humane working climate stems from many little actions and influences, too numerous to mention in detail. In the context of this paper, however, these may be summarized as follows:

1 Willingness on the part of 'the authorities' to allow panels to work on problems which panel members and other teachers perceive as real and worthy of attention.
2 Presence within the panel of able personnel in sufficient numbers to accomplish worthwhile tasks.
3 Freedom for panel members to express dissatisfaction with the current state of those affairs in schools, in LEAs, in the project or within the panel in which they have a legitimate interest.
4 Willingness on the part of all panel members to work together to achieve common ends through agreed means.
5 Recognition that many kinds of educationist can contribute to curriculum improvement.
6 An attitude of openmindedness and healthy scepticism about both what is traditional and what is new.
7 Absence of undue pressure by those in authority (whether within or outside the project) about matters which properly fall within the panel's decision.

## The professional centre leader

It will be apparent that if local curriculum development is to be successful, the centre must enjoy thoroughly competent professional leadership. In an age of specialists the centre leader needs to be a high-level general practitioner, able to understand and appreciate the concerns of class teacher, headteacher, LEA administrator, resource specialist, teacher trainer and higher education exponent. At the same time he needs to be good at establishing and maintaining productive and satisfying work relationships among persons drawn from several of these backgrounds but functioning as partners in a common task. To do this effectively he also needs a reasonable grounding in the several areas of academic study with which the centre's work is concerned.

Merely to list these attributes is to invite two questions: where are such masters of all the arts to be found? Why should such persons go into, and remain in, professional centre leadership? In the author's view the answer to the first question is that since few such persons are currently available we must set up leadership training programmes. It is, of course, true that if the James proposals for professional centre leaders are to be adopted courses need to be established through which potentially suitable applicants can accumulate the basic knowledge and rudiments of the skills they need for their work. Essentially, however, it is in the field that the professional centre leader, as general practitioner, accumulates wisdom, finesse, judgment, sensitivity and imaginative flair. So what is deceptive about the proposals for leadership training programmes is that real, worthwhile and acceptable projects have to be maintained so that such journeymen can learn the arts and can experience the humane working environment they must later seek to create elsewhere. And who is to lead *these* projects? Experience in the North West Project has shown the feasibility of university and LEA personnel working together on such a task. Once again, perhaps our most important finding has been that the centre leader who is a creative and enthusiastic member of a regional development panel is the one who induces in his centre a climate within which the teachers working there can also catch the spirit of creative endeavour.

Finally, why should so well qualified an exponent remain in professional centre work? It is obviously important to the education system that he do so; for in sociological terms he is a change agent, aiming to release more potential for innovation by promoting creative encounters among people interacting in flexible partnership.

But he is also a person, often with a family and always with career prospects, living in a society which tends to promote specialists to high-status posts, even where the work done in those posts approximates more to general than to specialist practice. That the James Committee has considered this point is obvious from its recommendations that the leader be called a warden, that he be given an independent role and that he enjoy at least senior lecturer status. These may well be necessary conditions for the post: but in the experience of the North West Project they are not sufficient conditions. Sufficient conditions are that the leader's work be emotionally and professionally satisfying, offering him also the experience of personal development and some evidence of the impact of his efforts upon schools. Because most of the project's centre leaders have experienced these rewards from their work I make bold to claim that were the James proposals accepted there would never be found lacking able teachers who were eager to make careers as professional centre leaders. Accordingly, I conclude that the James proposals for a network of professional centres, each under the leadership of a full-time professional warden are well-conceived, and merit the support of all proposed partners in third cycle teacher education.

*References*
SCHOOLS COUNCIL (1967) *Curriculum Development: Teachers' Groups and Centres* Working Paper 10 London: HMSO

# The contributors

Edward Britton
General Secretary, National Union of Teachers

Brian Cane
Deputy Principal, City of Sheffield College of Education

Lord Boyle
Vice-Chancellor, University of Leeds

Stanley Hewett
Secretary, Association of Teachers in Colleges and Departments of Education

Eric Hoyle
School of Education, University of Bristol

Lord James
Vice-Chancellor, University of York

Tony Light
Joint Secretary, Schools Council

Geoffrey Mattock
Senior Lecturer and Organizer of In-service Training, Institute of Education, University of Leeds

Eric Robinson
Deputy Director, North East London Polytechnic

Allan Rudd
Senior Lecturer and Organizing Tutor, School of Education, University of Manchester

John Taylor
Chief Education Officer, Leeds

Roger Watkins
Lecturer and Assistant Organizer of In-Service Training, Institute of Education, University of Leeds